Regimental History of the 1st Battalion 8th Punjab Regiment

Gosling Press

Copyright © N. M. Geoghegan & M.H.A. Campbell

This edition Copyright Gosling Press 2023

All rights reserved.

ISBN 978-1-874351-20-7 (Hardback)
ISBN 978-1-874351-21-4 (Paperback)

Gosling Press
www.goslingpress.co.uk

FOREWORD

The 89th Punjabis had a most distinguished record of service during the First World War. They have the unique distinction of claiming to have served in more theatres of war than any other unit of the British Empire. These included: Aden (Yemen), Egypt, Gallipoli, France, Mesopotamia, North West Frontier of India, Salonika (Greece), and the Russian Transcaucasia, where they served from 1918–20 as part of the British Expeditionary Force.

They are perhaps remembered unfortunately for their short deployment to Gallipoli, where after only two weeks they were withdrawn. The official reason given in the Official History was that the Brigade commander Maj. Gen. Sir H. V. Cox was opposed to the use of Mohammedan troops against the Turks. Sir Ian Hamilton in a letter to Lord Kitchener reinforced this on 2nd May by saying, "I do not propose to use the Mahametan Companies in the first fighting". Hamilton on the 14th of May followed this up in another cablegram, "sending back 69th and 89th Punjabis today as Cox does not think it wise to employ them in the firing line so close to Constantinople." Some of this thinking might be related to the mutiny by some companies of Muslmans from Eastern Punjab and Hindustan in Singapore in February 1915 although some of the reasons ascribed to the mutiny were a deeply unpopular British commanding officer, issues with recent promotions amongst the Indian ranks as well as the impending redeployment to Honk Kong. When the Class composition of the 89th Punjabis is considered in 1914 the Battalion comprised of 3 companies of Sikhs, 1 company of Brahmins, 1 company of Rajputs, 3 companies of Punjabi Musalmans, it is clear that Muslims made up less than fifty percent of the Battalion strength. It is perhaps more likely that the battalion was a casualty of Sir Ian Hamilton's desire to have more Ghurkhas on the peninsula. The idea of Muslim troops in the Battalions unreliability never came up again.

During the First World War there were 17 Victoria Crosses awarded to Indian Army personnel 11 of these to Indian officers or other ranks of these one was awarded to Naik Shahamad Khan a Punjabi Muslim in Mesopotamia on 12 to 13 April 1916. He was in charge of a machine gun covering a gap in the line very close to the enemy's trench, his citation reads:

> He was in charge of a machine gun section in an exposed position, in front of and covering a gap in our new line, within 150 yards of the enemy's entrenched position. He beat off three counter attacks and worked his gun single-handed after all his men, except two belt-fillers, had become casualties. For three hours, he held the gap under very heavy fire while it was being made secure. When his gun was knocked out by hostile fire, he and his two belt-fillers held their ground with rifles till ordered to withdraw. With three men sent to assist him he then brought back his gun, ammunition, and one severely wounded man unable to walk. Finally, he himself returned and removed all remaining arms and equipment except two shovels. But for his great gallantry and determination our line must have been penetrated by the enemy.

This regimental history has long been out of print and it is hoped that making it available once again will fill a gap in the accounts of a number campaigns.

Spelling in the original Regimental History can be inconsistent and sometimes eccentric (zig-zag in place of zigzag, etc.) this edition retains those inconsistencies

Regimental History
of the
1st Battalion
8th Punjab Regiment

Col. N. M. Geoghegan

&

Capt. M.H.A. Campbell

Edited by John Wilson

BRIGADIER-GENERAL L. W. Y. CAMPBELL, C.M.G.,
Colonel of the Battalion.

PREFACE

This record of the battalion's War Service is the result of the combined labours of Colonel N. M. Geoghegan, D.S.O. and captain M. H. A. Campbell, O.B.E. These two were the only officers who served continuously with the Battalion from November 1914, when it left India, till its return from Constantinople in September 1920.

This book has been compiled chiefly from Regimental Records, War Diary, old war maps, sketches and photographs. But the authors also wish to thank all of those who have so readily helped them with anecdotes of personal experiences and other information.

J. Scruby, Lieut-Colonel,
Cmdt. 1st Bn. 8th Punjab Regt.

CONTENTS

	INTRODUCTION	1
I	MOBILISATION	3
II	THE CAPTURE OF FORT TURBA	7
III	EGYPT NOVEMBER, 1914 TO APRIL 1915	14
IV	GALLIPOLI – MAY, 1915	21
V	FRANCE JUNE TO DECEMBER 1915	29
VI	MESOPOTAMIA JANUARY TO AUGUST 1916	53
VII	NORTH-WEST FRONTIER OF INDIA 1916–1917	82
VIII	MESOPOTAMIA DECEMBER 1917 TO OCTOBER 1918	92
IX	Salonika And The Army Of The Black Sea November 1918 To October 1920	104
X	Appendices	113

Illustrations and maps

Brigadier-General L.W.Y. Campbell, C.M.G., Colonel of The Battalion	iv
Group of Officers, Dinapore	5
Sketch of Sheikh Sayed	9
Sketch of El-Kantara, February, 1915	18
Sketch of Cape Helles	25
Sketch of Trenches Near Geoghegan's Bluff, Gallipoli	27
Photographs of Trenches Near Neuve Chapelle	37
Sketch of Trenches Near Neuve Chapelle	51
Colonel N. M. Geoghegan, D.S.O.	54
Photographs of Mesopotamia	59
Subedar Shahmed Khan, V.C.	70
Sketch of Beit Aiessa Trenches	76
Sketch of Mesopotamia Near Kut	79
Group of Officers of 89th, August, 1916	83
Photographs Taken on The March To Chitral	88
Group of Officers of 89th, November, 1917	91
Sketch of Lower Mesopotamia	96
Photograph Taken When With Army of The Black Sea	107
Sketch of Caucasia	112

INTRODUCTION

The 1st Battalion, 8th Punjab Regiment was raised at Masulipatam by Captain Macleod in 1798, during the war with Tipoo Sultan. It was originally known as the Macleod Ki Paltan, or 29th Regiment Madras Infantry. This Battalion was mustered out on October 15th, 1893, and was reconstituted as a Punjabi battalion at Meiktila from Burma Military Police on October 16th, 1893, as the 29th (7th Burma Battalion) Regiment of Madras Infantry.

In December, 1896, the Battalion moved to Fort Stedman, where it was stationed for three years. From December, 1899, until January, 1902, it spent in Bhamo, after which it moved to Mandalay. In 1901, it became known as the 29th Burma Infantry, and in 1903, under the new renumbering by Lord Kitchener, as the 89th Punjabis.

In October, 1904, the Battalion left Mandalay for Rangoon, from which station it had to supply a detachment for Port Blair in the Andaman Islands. In March, 1907, the Battalion was again stationed at Mandalay, where it remained for over three years.

From November, 19th, until May 1911, the 89th Punjabis were stationed at Myitkyina. During their stay here, two double companies, under Major Campbell, were sent on a punitive expedition in Pienma territory. This was the nearest approach to anything like active service that the Battalion, as such, ever experienced before the Great War of 1914–18.

In May, 1911, the 89th found themselves back again in Meiktila, where they remained until March, 1914. From Meiktila they moved to India, and in April, 1914, arrived at Dinapore, in which station they were still serving when war broke out in August.

The record of the 89th Punjabis during the Great War of 1914–18 is one of which all ranks may be justly proud. Since its reconstruction in 1893, on the disbandment of the old 29th Madras Infantry, the Battalion, as such had had no opportunity of seeing active service. In fact, with the exception of a few officers and men who had been transferred from the Burma Military Police, there was none who had seen a shot fired in anger.

It was, therefore, with no little excitement that the Battalion received, on October 11th, 1914, orders to mobilise for service. That the Regiment should have acquitted itself so well is largely due to the spirit of never doing things by halves, which was inculcated into all ranks by the former Commanding Officers, who were no longer with the Battalion to see the results of their unremitting labours in peace.

To no other single battalion, British or Indian, was it given to serve on so many fronts as did the 89th Punjabis. In South-West Arabia, in Egypt, in Gallipoli, in France, in Mesopotamia, on the North-West Frontier of India, again in Mesopotamia, in Salonika, in the Caucasus, and finally at Constantinople with the Army of the Black Sea, the Battalion was called upon for active service; and in all of these its reputation for gallantry and efficiency was always high.

Paradoxically, the fortune that gave the Battalion such wide experience in many theatres of war was a misfortune that prevented it from gaining its full quota of rewards and honours, since, as soon as the Battalion became known to its G.O.C., fate called on it to start afresh under new ones. In spite of all, however, the Battalion throughout maintained the best traditions of the Service.

At the time of the outbreak of the war, battalions in India were still organised under the eight company system with four double companies in each India battalion. And, although the names "platoon" and "company" were used in France in 1915 and in Mesopotamia in 1916, the Battalion was not reorganised until the end of 1916 when at Nowshera. It was then that No.1 Double Company, composed of A and B Companies, was organised into one company as A Company, C and D Companies as C Company, E and F Companies as F Company, G and H Companies as H Company, and Headquarters organised into one company, named Z.

Chapter I

MOBILISATION

When the news of the declaration of war between Great Britain and Germany reached India, there were few, if any, of us in Dinapore who thought that the Battalion would ever be called upon to take an active part. The most that appeared possible was garrison duty in some overseas station, in relief of British regiments called away for the sterner duty of war.

In accordance, however, with orders received, all officers and other ranks were recalled from leave, and the Battalion settled down to normal routine work. Later, the news filtered through that two Indian divisions were to proceed overseas. The destination of these divisions was thought to be only Egypt, but, anyhow, that was a stage nearer the theatre of war. On August 14th, orders were received to despatch drafts of I Indian officer and 197 other ranks to the 9th Bhopal Infantry. These were rapidly got ready and despatched to join that battalion under Major Geoghegan. This officer had visions of attaching himself permanently with the draft and so going overseas with the 9th Bhopals. He was not, however permitted to do so, as the 9th Bhopals already had their full complement of British officers. And, also, as it turned out, only the Indian officer and 64 men of our draft were required after all. In accordance with Regimental custom, only the very best men of the Battalion were picked to form drafts. It is regretted that no detailed account of the exploits of these men is available. But more than one British officer who served with the 9th Bhopal Infantry has spoken most highly of the work of Jemadar Ramsurat Misr and the men of the 89th draft.

On Sunday, October 11th, 1914, a telegram was received from Presidency Brigade Headquarters, warning the Battalion for active service. There was intense excitement amongst all ranks. Actual orders were received on Thursday, the 15th, to mobilise with 10 percent reinforcements and to call upon the 90th Punjabis to complete any deficiencies. Our 120 reservists were called up, but, as the Battalion had been much depleted by the despatch of drafts to the 9th Bhopals, and to various signal companies, it was found necessary to ask the 90th to supply 2 Indian officers and 77 other ranks. This party joined the Battalion on the 19th, and a Brahmin Indian Officer from the 1st Brahmins joined two days later.

Mobilisation was complete on Friday, the 23rd, just eight days after the actual order to mobilise had been received. The Battalion had been re-armed throughout with the Mark III Short L. E., and issued with 1903 pattern bayonet. All these, as well as other mobilisation stores, had to drawn from arsenal.

Early on the 27th, the advance party, under Lieutenant G. E. Masters left for Karachi, followed at midday by the rest of the Battalion (see Appendix I). The Battalion fell in on the parade ground at 1000 hours and, after farewell address s by the Regimental Grunthi, Moulvie, and Pandit, marched to the station for active service, from which it was not return until it had seen many vicissitudes, much hard fighting, and had lost many of its best officers and men.

The Battalion had orders to embark at Karachi, which place was reached at 0400 hours on October 31st. Here we were joined by Captain J. D. Strong, 90th Punjabis, who served with the Battalion until its withdrawal from Gallipoli, where he stayed on to serve with the 14th Sikhs. He was shortly afterwards severely wounded, losing the sight of both eyes.

GROUP OF BRITISH OFFICERS AT DINAPORE, OCTOBER, 1914.

Back Row:—Captain Fielding, I.M.S. Captain Janes. Colonel Campbell. Colonel Murray. Major Geoghegan. Major Prentis.
Seated:—Captain Wood. Lieut. Rohde. Captain Chapman. Captain Crawford.
On Ground:—Captain Scruby. Lieut. Masters. 2nd-Lieut. Campbell.

The Battalion found itself brigaded with the 14th Sikhs, 69th Punjabis, and the 1st/6th Gurkha Rifles, to form the 29th Indian Infantry Brigade, I.E.F., F, under Brigadier-General H. V. Cox, C.B., C.S.I., C.I.E. No one could have wished for a finer lot of battalions to serve with, or for a better Brigadier to serve under.

On November 1st, the Battalion embarked on H.T. *Edavana,* together with a detachment of the 69th Punjabis and Brigade Headquarters.

The *Edavana* left Kiamari Docks on the 2nd, and sailed in a convoy, with nine other vessels, under escort of H.M.S. *Duke of Edinburgh*. On the 5th, this convoy joined another one, of twenty-six ships, from Bombay, under the escort of H.M.S. *Swiftsure* and R.I.M.S. *Hardinge*. That enormous convoy, stretching almost from horizon to horizon, was a sight never to be forgotten by those who saw it – a sight eloquent of the fact that Britain ruled the waves.

Captains W. L. B. Chapman and W. R. James were left in India in charge of the Depot. It was for them a depressing sight to see the Battalion go on service while they remained behind. Both, however, subsequently joined

the Battalion in the field, and both were wounded. The work that they did at the Depot has played a larger part in the success of the Battalion than any at that time imagined was possible.

Chapter II

THE CAPTURE OF FORT TURBA

Shortly after joining the convoy from Bombay, H.T. *Edavana* detached from the main convoy and ran at increased speed for Aden. Here Major Bradshaw, Intelligence Officer, embarked, and certain naval ratings were transferred to the Edavana. These proceedings tended to confirm the suspicion, which had arisen in the ship, that the unit was to form part of a special mission.

We left Aden on November 9th, in company with two other transports carrying the remainder of the 29th Brigade, escorted by H.M.S. *Duke of Edinburgh*. The same evening, orders were issued for landing on the east coast of Sheikh Sayed Peninsula near Jebel Basis. The Turkish fort of Turba is situated on one of the number of hills forming the peninsula overlooking the Island of Perim, and, in 1914, contained guns of sufficient power to be a permanent menace to the island and to all shipping passing through the straits. Our objective, therefore, was the capture and destruction of the fort and more especially of the heavy guns. There were a couple of small villages on the peninsula, but only local Arabs could exist on the totally inadequate and very brackish water supply. The Turkish garrison, although composed of men inured to the conditions of South-West Arabia, were obliged to get their drinking water, by sea, from Dubab, a place some twenty miles up the coast.

All necessary orders were issued concerning disembarkation and advanced guard, but, when the transports arrived in position about 0130 hours on the 10th, the naval reconnaissance party reported a heavy surf and a rocky beach. This, combined with a strong east wind and pitch darkness, rendered the operation unsafe. So the scheme was abandoned, and the men were dismissed at 0245 hours. Fresh plans were then made for a bombardment of Fort Turba by daylight by H.M.S. *Duke of Edinburgh*, to be followed later by a landing of troops on the west side of the peninsula.

The bombardment began at 0615 hours on the 10th, and to those watching from the transports it appeared as though nothing would be left to attack when their turn came. They were yet to realise, both here and later at Gallipoli, what a slight effect the naval gun fire of the period had on an enemy entrenched on shore.

At 10 00 hours, H.M.S. *Duke of Edinburgh* took up position to cover the landing of troops with gunfire. Operation orders having been receive detailing the 89th Punjabis and a half battalion of the 69th Punjabis to]and, the disembarkation began at 1035 hours. The covering party, under Captain Engledue, including the Regimental Scouts, reached the shore at 1050 hours, and seized Hill 70, practically unopposed. The enemy had opened fire on the beach with shrapnel, but the bursts were too high to do much harm. The few enemy in the village retired as Captain Engledue's force advanced, and the disembarkation continued under cover of his party.

By 1135 hours, the enemy had occupied and opened long-range rifle fire from Camp Hill. Shrapnel fire had continued from the ridge south of Camp Hill, but, although the ranging had improved, the landing parties were still working almost immune from danger. The telegraph line running near the shore was now cut, and a regimental aid post established under the shelter of Hill 70.

The Machine Gun Section (two guns) came into action on Hill 70,

Rough sketch of Sheikh Sayed Peninsula

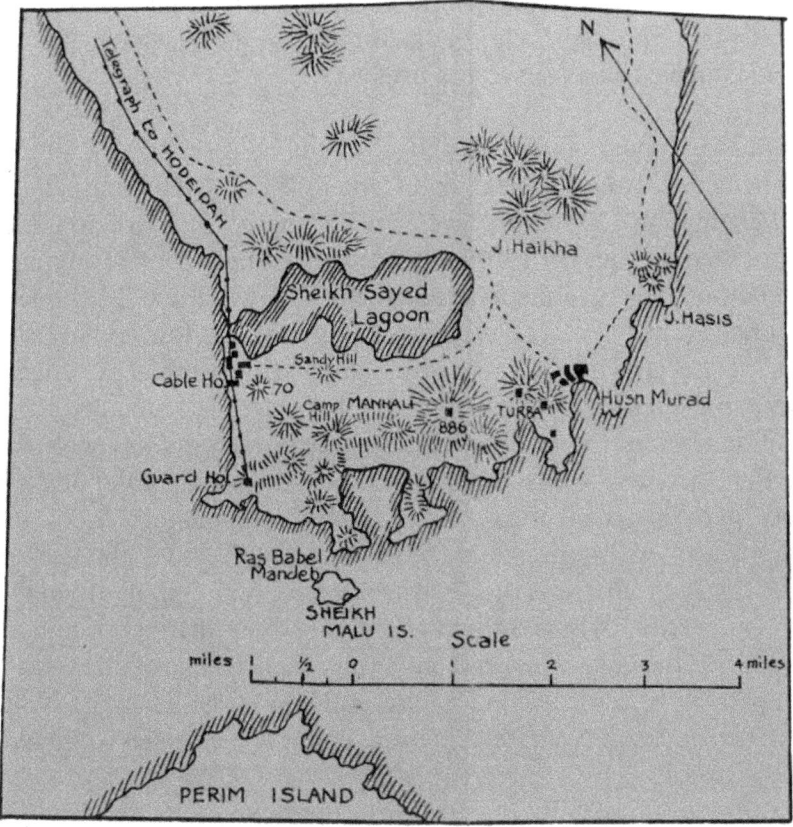

strengthening the position of the covering force, but, as things turned out the guns never got any very definite target.

The O.C. 69th Punjabis, with a small force and one machine gun, had effected a landing farther south, and had advanced towards the south of Camp Hill. He now asked for support, but, as the Brigade Commander had given strict orders that two double companies were to be collected at Hill 70, and this number was not yet complete, no assistance could be given at the moment. In addition, the distance was too great for support by anything but positions before the troops could get home with the bayonet. For long-range fire, which, in the circumstances, was considered useless.

By 1245 hours, Nos. 1 and 2 Double Companies, under Lieutenant- Colonel Murray and Captain Wood, were complete at Hill 70, and by 1300 hours half of 'F' Company had arrived under Major Geoghegan. By 1400 hours, the machine guns, G Company and half of F being concentrated at Hill 70, Nos. 1 and 2 Double Companies and the scouts advanced against the low hills north-east of Camp Hill and against Camp Hill itself. The enemy opposed the advance by rifle and gun fire, but evacuated their positions before the troops could get home with the bayonet. For the first thousand yards, the advance was over loose sand and the latter part up naked rocky ridges similar to many parts of the Indian frontier. As the enemy's fire became effective, the system of advance by alternate rushes was adopted, and, greatly owing to the excellence of the previous training and the good mutual timing of the advances and covering fire, the casualties were comparatively few, Second Lieutenant M. H. A. Campbell, the first officer casualty in the Battalion, being one of those wounded.

The first group of hills being now in our possession, the G.O.C., who had arrived at Hill 70, ordered no further advance to be made, and called for reports from the points occupied. Lieutenant-Colonel Murray, who was on the north-eastern slopes of Camp Hill, reported that the enemy had retired, but that there was still a large body of the enemy on his left front. Captain Wood, with no 2 Double Company, who had captured one field gun, two prisoners, and much ammunition and other stores on Camp Hill, continued his advance, and later occupied Fort Turba without opposition.

Except for these two double companies and half of F and half of H, the Battalion now moved from Hill 70 to Sandy Hill a low mound on the path to the north-east of Camp Hill. Colonel Murray reported the enemy retiring north-east, so Major

Geoghegan pushed on with his Double Company in pursuit. The machine guns tried long-range fire, but with no effect, as the enemy were practically out of range. A large number of enemy were found by Major Geoghegan retiring along the east coast of the peninsula from Fort Turba and the village past the three mounds, near Jebel Haikah, where a party of snipers had been left to cover their withdrawal. Leaving a half-company to deal with the enemy on Jebel Haikah, Major Geoghegan pushed on in the vain hope of cutting off at least the tail of the column. At length they had to resort to pursuit by fire, and it was only possible to get off a few effective rounds. The only visible "bag" was one mule!

Major Geoghegan's party now built sangars on a site commanding the road from the fort and the village, but well clear of the surrounding hills, with a view to spending the night. A report to that effect was sent to Battalion Headquarters. The half-company watching Jebel Haikah was then called in, and, just as it joined Major Geoghegan, orders were received from Battalion Headquarters to withdraw to Sandy Hill. The whole party then withdrew, having first knocked down the sangars.

That night, Nos. 1 and 2 Double Companies remained in their positions near Fort Turba, and furnished their own battle outposts. The remainder of the Battalion concentrated at Sandy Hill, posted battle outposts, and reorganised.

Next morning, four companies of the 14th Sikhs landed and took over the outer protective duties. The 23rd Pioneers, from Aden, disembarked and at once began demolition and salvage work, their job being to complete the demolition of the armament of the fort. Though immense craters had been blown in the glacis of the fort by the naval bombardment, the fort itself and its armament, except for one big gun, were practically undamaged.

The G.O.C. published the following order:-
> The G.O.C. is very pleased with the good spirit with which the operations at Turba were carried out. The nature of the task made it by no means easy, and the G.O.C. thanks all ranks for their good work which made the operations successful.

Some of the draft of the 90th Punjabis did very well in this action, and the C.O., in writing to the O.C. 90th Punjabis, said, 'I was very pleased with the splendid way in which your fellows worked, and greatly regret to have to report the death of one of them.'

Although the fighting in this action was not very severe, nor were the casualties heavy, the account has been given in some detail because it was the first time the Battalion had been under fire since its reconstruction in 1893.

The original intention had been to effect this landing in the ship's

boats, manned by Lascar crews assisted by sepoys. Luckily the G.O.C. insisted on the necessity for naval assistance, and a number of naval ratings were transferred to the *Edavana* at Aden. In spite of the fact that the ship's boats had been filled with water for some days before landing, they leaked so badly that one foundered altogether on the first trip to the shore and two others were so water-logged as to be practically useless. Moreover, even with the assistance of the naval steam-launches to tow the boats ashore and the addition of naval boats and pinnaces holding from twenty to seventy-five fully-armed men, it took from 1035 till 1400 hours to get 75 percent of the Battalion ashore. There was a fair sea running, which made the transfer of men from the ocean-going steamer to small boats a slow job. No special gangways had been rigged for this purpose, as a light-draught steamer had been ordered to act as tender between the transport and the shallower water inshore. This vessel did not arrive, however until too late to take part in the disembarkation. Our men were evidently much impressed by the behaviour of the naval ratings detailed to help us to land on the beach. For on the 11th, after our re-embarkation, as the naval ratings were leaving the *Edavana* to return to the *Duke of Edinburgh*, the sepoys) quite spontaneously, gave them a hearty cheer.

For first aid to Second Lieutenant Campbell under fire and for carrying him back to a place of safety, No.290 Sepoy Bur Singh and No.2028 Sepoy Buta Singh received the I.D.S.M. afterwards.

No.2131 Sepoys Dasaunda Singh also received the I.D.S.M. for similar conduct. The names of the following Indian officer and other ranks were also brought to notice:-

Subedar Thakur Singh.

No.1638	Havildar Painde Khan.
No.1334	Havildar Ghulam Mohd.
No.1240	Havildar Bagga Singh.
No.1554	Naik Karm Ilahi.
No.2206	Lance-Naik Isher Singh.
No.1860	Lance-Naik Sucher Singh.
No.2120	Lance-Naik Kishun Singh.
No.2020	Sepoy Karm Singh.

The total casualties sustained by the Battalion in this action were: Died of wounds, 1 other rank; wounded, 1 British officer, and 7 other ranks.

While these operations were in progress, the remainder of the convoy from Bombay and Karachi steamed past. The Battalion, however, re-embarked shortly after the 14th Sikhs had landed. The *Edavana*, being allowed to proceed at full speed with the wounded to Suez, soon re-passed the convoy and was the first ship in.

Chapter III

EGYPT NOVEMBER, 1914 TO APRIL 1915

The battalion disembarked at Suez on November 16th 1914, proceeded at once in two trains to Port Said, and took over the defence of that place from the Highland Light Infantry. Nos. 3 and 4 Double Companies went on outpost duties on the east of the Canal with headquarters at the salt works and the canal works respectively, while numerous guards were furnished in and around the town by the other half battalion

As the remainder of the Brigade arrived, the local guards were taken over by other troops, and the whole Battalion was concentrated on the east bank with Headquarters at the salt works. The Brigade was now distributed as follows: the 89th, east of the Canal on outpost duty; the 69th Punjabis, farther down the Canal, between the 8th and 14th kilo, with picquets on the east bank and supports on the west; the 14th Sikhs and 1st/6th Gurkhas, in reserve at Port Said.

In the event of attack, H.M.S. *Swiftsure* was to move to a point in the Canal south of Port Said, to cover our right flank, whilst H.M.S. *Proserpine* was to protect our left flank from the sea.

All troops were called upon to furnish large working parties daily for the construction of field works, and the Royal Engineers cut

the bank of the salt works canal, with a view to flooding the desert east of Port Said. The rush of water was so great, that disaster threatened the whole bank until the sea came to our rescue. A violent storm arose on November 26th, and the sea broke through, a few miles up the coast, flooding the whole country, and so reducing the force of the water at the breach in the bank. The breach was promptly refilled and the bank restored to its original condition. The sea had completed in a few hours the inundation which it had been calculated would take three weeks. Incidentally, the same storm played havoc with all the beautiful redoubts and other works built by the units of the Brigade. These were, of necessity chiefly composed of salt and sand. The construction of
fresh works kept all units busily employed during December, units taking it in turn to furnish outposts.

Some other incidents of note were the capture of a suspicious ship on the sea-shore by Captain Scruby; the sighting of an enemy patrol .on January 7th about a mile out in the desert by a Gurkha patrol; a meeting held at El-Kantara on December 26th to which a number of Indian officers went, to meet the Aga Khan; the departure of Captain Scruby on January 3rd to act as Machine Gun Instructor to the 3rd Brigade Australian Contingent at Cairo; and the return to duty on January 9th of Lieutenant M. H. A. Campbell.

On January 9th, the Battalion, having been relieved by the 3rd Brahmans, moved by rail to El-Kantara, where it took over part of the defences from the 93rd Burma Infantry. During the next ten days, much work was put in on the defences of El-Kantara, the Battalion being responsible, principally, for the southern face, the Cemetery Redoubt, and a share of the outpost work.

On January 13th, Second Lieutenants Peto and Hasluck, I.A.R.O. joined the Battalion from the Ceylon Contingent. The former officer was subsequently severely wounded in Mesopotamia, and eventually had to be invalided out of the Service; the latter unfortunately was killed in Gallipoli while serving with the 14th Sikhs.

On the 21st, the Brigade made a reconnaissance along the El-Arish Road, and entrenched a position at Hill 40, about four miles east of the Canal, as a strongpoint for the infantry of the covering force which was sent out daily in support of the cavalry and camelry patrols. These patrols were fired on by the enemy on the 24th.

On the return from outpost duty on the morning of the 25th, the O.C. No.3 Double Company reported having seen two of the enemy north of the outpost line. However, the same day the Brigade proceeded to Ballah, the next station south of El-Kantara, to practise reinforcing that post. The usual covering party was out at Hill 40, and only No.3 Double Company and half of No.1 Double Company remained in camp. The enemy selected this moment to appear in force from the direction of Bir-el-Duweida, so the Brigade was hurriedly recalled. The Battalion was back in El-Kantara by 1230 hours, and a portion of the Brigade engaged the enemy; but, beyond furnishing two escorts for armed tugs, the Battalion was not employed. From cavalry and aeroplane reports, it was understood that there were not more than 800 infantry and 300 mounted enemy opposing El-Kantara.

On the 27th, Nos. 3 and 4 Double Companies formed part of the covering force, but, though the enemy mounted and dismounted troops were seen, they only exchanged a few shots. The same day, Captain Scruby rejoined from Cairo.

The morning of the 28t h, a Turkish patrol tried to penetrate our outpost line. The party, guided by the line of telegraph poles, blundered in between Nos. 4 and 5 picquets. The picquets, manned by the 14th Sikhs, opened fire, and the Turks withdrew, leaving three or four dead. The next day, by Brigadier-General Cox's order, the line of telegraph poles was slightly altered, so as to lead direct into No.5 picquet. That night, an armed tug was fired on about a mile north of Ballah, fortunately with no result. On the 30th, the strength of the outposts was increased from one double company to half a battalion.

On February 2nd, there had been a sandstorm all day, and the night was cloudy. That evening, Nos. 3 and 4 Double Companies

went on outpost duty, under Majors Geoghegan and Prentis. No.3 Double Company was holding picquets Nos. 1, 2 and 3; and No.4 Double Company Nos. 4, 5 and 6 picquets. Major Prentis was in No.5 picquet. At 0130 hours, the Turks sent up many red and white rocket signals. At 0400 hours, No.5 picquet's patrols fell back with the report that the enemy were advancing in numbers. About 0430 hours, they came on in the pitch-dark led by the telegraph poles straight into No.5 picquet. They advanced in
several lines, shoulder to shoulder, and, in trying to outflank the picquet, parties ran up against Nos. 4 and 6 picquets. About 0500 hours, No.2 Double Company was ordered out in support, as No.4 Double Company was getting short of ammunition. Behind them followed the C.O. and Adjutant. When day broke, those of the enemy who could extricate themselves from in front of No.5 picquet suffered many casualties from shrapnel fire from H.M.S. *Swiftsure*. These casualties included the headquarters of a Turkish regiment. A few of the enemy
were still visible in front of the picquet wire, and these were rounded up by the picquet at the point of the bayonet. Much to our surprise, no fewer than 32 unwounded and 4 wounded prisoners were found, dug in, in front of us, also 20 dead in the entanglement. When the daily covering party passed through the outpost line, No.4 and No.2 Double Companies returned to camp, leaving No.3 in support of Tel-el-Ahmar, which was receiving attention from a force of Turks to the south-east. At 0730 hours, No.1 Double Company were ordered out to attack this force, assisted by the 26th Mountain Battery, but could not come to grips with them because of the flooded nature of the country. However, they stayed out there until 1800 hours the same evening. It was here that No.2131 Sepoy Dasaunda

Singh again distinguished himself. Nine times he brought up ammunition to No.1 Double Company from the camp. On each occasion, he carried back a killed or wounded man on his back to the dressing station, which was over 800 yards to the rear. To perform the journey more quickly, he removed his boots, as the going was over heavy, loose sand. On each occasion he was exposed to heavy fire from the enemy. At 1330 hours, No.2 Double Company went out again, this time to reinforce the garrison of Tel-el- Ahmar. At 1700 hours, No.3 Double Company

Rough Sketch of El-Kantara Defences in February 1915

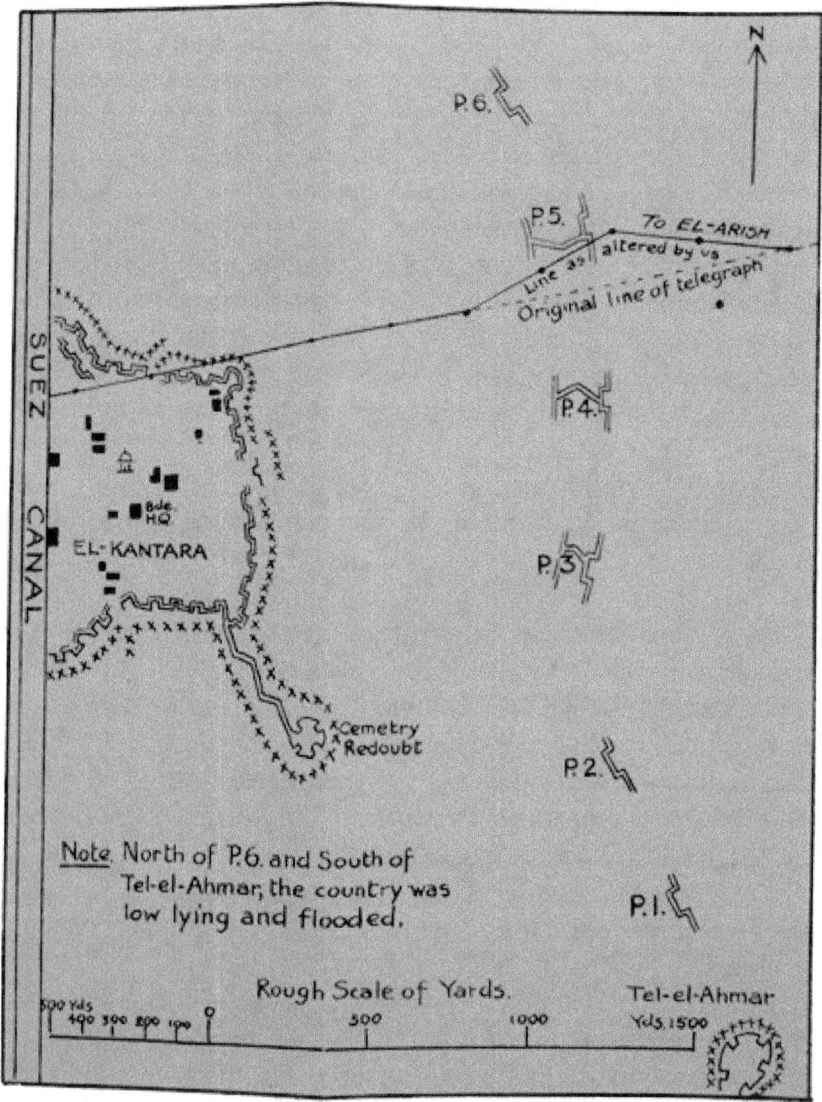

relieved No.1 Double Company, which returned to camp. Nos 2 and 3 Double Companies remained out all night, the former in Tel-el-Ahmar Redoubt and the latter between that post and the Canal. The enemy withdrew that night, and on the morning of the

4th had finally disappeared. During the sever l engagements on the 3rd, our casualties were 1 British officer (Captain Engledue) slightly wounded, and of the rank and file 4 men were killed and 22 wounded.

One incident which caused delight in the Battalion occurred during the attack on the outposts on the morning of the 3rd. A Turk, evidently trying to desert, came up to No.2 picquet in the dark shouting out "Mahmoud! Mahmoud!" The sentry, a Brahman, halted him, and a couple of men were just about to go and secure him, when he attempted to bolt past through the picquet line. The sentry, at a word from the Indian officer, fired at him as he was running past, shooting him dead through the heart. The sentry had recently classified as a third-class shot in Dinapore!

On February 5th, a congratulatory order was received from the G.O.C. in C. of the Forces in Egypt (see Appendix II).

From February 6th to 8th, improvements were carried out on the defences along the Canal. On the 9th, the Battalion took over the post at Ballah and all the intervening posts along the Canal and at El-Kap, we remained there in detachments until March 1st, when the Battalion was again concentrated at El-Kantara. Here we were employed on road-making, maintenance of defences: and ordinary training until the first week in April.

On April 7th, when No.1 Double Company was out on the daily covering force, the cavalry reported 1,200 enemy to the south of Hill 40! At the same time, one of our infantry patrols, which went out at dawn each morning along the banks of the Canal, reported suspicious traces of men and camels and a broken packing-case about two miles north of El-Kantara. Putting two and two together, the G.O.C. stopped all traffic through the Canal, and
with the help of the Navy dragged the water near the spot. Eventually a small mine was caught in the net. A burly A.B., who was told to make it fast to a small rowing-boat he was in, mistaking his orders, bent over it, took it in his arms and hoisted it into the boat. No one, however, was brave enough to take the mine out of the boat again, and so it was taken back to El-

Kantara, where it was dragged ashore, boat and all, and destroyed by the Sappers and Miners.

In the afternoon, one of our aeroplanes marked down a squadron of enemy cavalry two and a half miles north-west of Bir-el-Duweidar.

On April 15th, the Battalion moved to the west bank of the Canal, and, on the 18th left by rail for Port Said en route to the Dardanelles.

Chapter IV

GALLIPOLI – MAY, 1915

A Brigade depot under Lieutenant White I.A.R.O., attached to the 69th Punjabis, was detailed to remain in Egypt, and, on our arrival at Port Said, all surplus stores were lodged in the S. & T. go-downs.

On the morning of April 26th, the personnel of the battalion embarked on H.T. *Ajax*, and sailed the next morning. The transport and officers' chargers followed later in H.T. *Japanese Prince*.

Cape Helles was reached on the morning of the 29th. Heavy fighting was taking place on shore, and a very fair view of the first advance against Krithia was obtained from the ship.

The Battalion disembarked on the 30th, by lighter, at the River Clyde landing on 'V Beach', and moved into bivouac on the cliffs between that and 'W beach'. The first casualty occurred as the battalion left the beach. A shell falling bear the column threw up a lot of earth. A piece of sod entered a sepoy's open mouth, and, lodging in his throat, would most certainly have suffocated him had not medical assistance been immediately at hand. An Indian transport corps was found on the beach, so that, as we were the first Indian unit to land, it was not very difficult to borrow some carts to help with our meagre kits and stores. The men were each carrying three days rations on their persons, and, owing to the heavy British casualties of the previous days, officers found ample rations for themselves on shore.

On May 1st, although under shellfire all day, the Battalion did not take part in any actual fighting, but remained in their bivouacs on the cliff between 'V' and 'W' Beaches. All ranks remained fully accoutred the whole night, as heavy fighting was taking place in the front line. In fact, this was the beginning of the first great Turkish counter-attack, which lasted, off and on, for five days. The enemy opened with shell fire about 2200 hours, and about half an hour later delivered a succession of charges. They succeeded in breaking through in places, to the second line, but where there held up. At dawn, the entire British line advanced and drove the Turks back on to their machine guns, which, in turn, held up our advance.

On May 2nd, the 29th Indian Brigade advanced into reserve to the 29th Division. The advance was carried out in artillery formation. Afterwards, officers and small parties of scouts and guides from each unit went forward to the front line trenches to learn the geography of them and to establish touch with their new comrades of the 29th Division. Curiously enough, old friends from Burma and Dinapore were almost the first to be met. The Battalion bivouacked for the night about 800 yards north-west of Stone Bridge, and officers went round the second line trenches by night. On the morning of the 3rd, officers and scouts made further reconnaissance's while the Battalion improved and continued the trenches near 'V Beach'. The regimental transport, under Captain Scruby, rejoined the same day. Fatigues were employed all the afternoon and evening, clearing stores and rations from 'W Beach'. Late that night, the Battalion settled down in bivouacs on the cliffs.

At 0530 hours on the 4th, the Battalion, with the 14th Sikhs, was ordered out in support of the French left, where their line joined the British. On arrival at Stone Bridge, information was received that the situation had been restored, so we returned to the cliffs. The Battalion was employed all day on fatigues ma king and improving roads, landing and moving stores, helping to land guns, and to pull them up to the top of the cliffs.

At 1900 hours, the Brigade moved into bivouac near Stone Bridge, in support. of the French left. The Battalion was located in front of some rising ground occupied by a battery of French 75s. These guns fired continuously all night. However, after four days
and nights of continuous work with little or no sleep, most of us were undisturbed by the noise, and made the most of a comparatively quiet night.

The next day saw more fatigue work for us. About 400 were employed in improving the trenches of the 87th Brigade, and the remainder were employed on the beach. At 2200 hours, Nos. 3 and 4 Double Companies and Machine Gun Section moved up with the 14th Sikhs in support of the 88th Brigade.

On the morning of the 6th, Brigade Headquarters and the 6th Gurkhas arrived in the same neighbourhood. During the afternoon, this force advanced three-quarters of a mile, and occupied a line of trenches. At 1900 hours, orders were received to advance still farther and take up the position just vacated by the 88th Brigade. This position was occupied with much difficulty, because of the darkness. Captain Strong and three sections of E Company went still farther forward in close support of part of the 88th Brigade. These positions were maintained all the next day, covering an advance made by the 88th Brigade.

On the morning of May 8th, Captain Strong and his party rejoined the Double Company. At 1900 hours, Nos. 3 and 4 Double Companies had to move along the trench to the west, and take up a position from the sea to the ravine (Saghir Dere) running up from Gully Beach. The trenches were so crowded with New Zealand troops, and also with wounded men, that it was necessary to make this flank movement the open within close rifle range of the enemy, and mostly on the skyline. Luckily, the move took place during a temporary lull in the fighting, and was also favoured by the gathering dusk. Only six casualties were sustained. We now collected at the ravine, and found ourselves in a maze of half constructed trenches, full of abandoned kit and equipment, and altogether in a filthy condition. About 2300 hours, the trenches became congested with South Wales Borderers, who had been sent back from the first line trenches, just in front for a temporary rest.

Early the next morning, we handed the trenches over to the South

Wales Borderers and concentrated in the ravine. At 1000 hours, we were ordered to remain in the *nullah*, as the 29th Indian Brigade was to relieve the 87th Brigade. At 1630 hours, the battalion took over some trenches astride the ravine from the Inniskilling Fusiliers. The enemy kept up a heavy fire from 2100 hours till 0100 hours, but did not press home any attack on the battalion front. After 0100 hours they kept us a desul6tory fire with machine guns and snipers.

The morning of May 10th was comparatively quiet. The day was spent in improving trenches and communications and trying to locate enemy machine guns and snipers. One of the latter was particularly active against F Company throughout the day. It was on this day that, on looking back from Geoghegan's Bluff towards our own machine guns, the conspicuous nature of the pugree was noticed. This disadvantage was got over by the Sikhs making use of their comforters, and other men wearing the Balaclava cap rolled up. During the morning, half of C Company came up as reinforcement from Stone Bridge. After dusk, a covering party was furnished for some Australian Engineers, who went forward and fixed up an entanglement across the ravine between the picquet posts. Half of C Company, under Captain Scruby, moved up on the left of F Company, which was more or less unprotected.

About 2200 hours, heavy rifle fire broke out against F Company trench, continuing practically all night, and at 0300 hours a similar fire was directed against No.4 Double Company. All ranks stood to arms, as it was thought that the enemy were making preparations for an attack. During the night, Major Prentis (with No.4 Double Company) was severely wounded, and Captain Scruby was sent up to take command in his place. Shortly after daylight, Captain Scruby reported that a new enemy trench had

Rough Sketch of Cape Helles

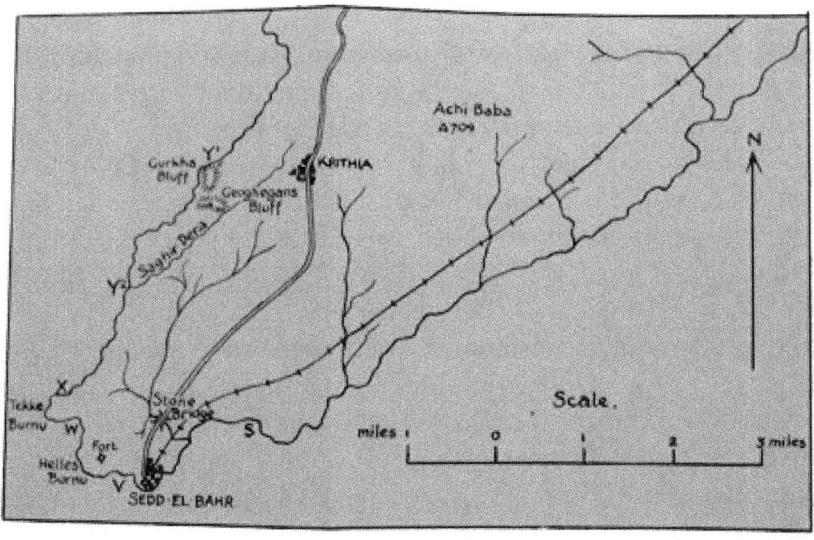

been made during the night about 400 yards to his front and that of F Company. Thus the heavy rifle fire of the night before was explained. However, we soon scored a point by spotting a sniper perched up in a tree about 100 yards from F Company trench. He was successfully "dropped". Again that evening, at 2000 hours, the enemy opened up, this time with shrapnel as well as rifle fire.

Captain Scruby reported a party of Turks advancing down the ravine. The 7th Manchesters, at this time moving up the ravine to relieve the New Zealanders on the right, detached one platoon, who were formed across the ravine with fixed bayonets to be ready to charge should the ravine picquets be forced. The Turks did not attempt to get through, and the platoon was withdrawn about an hour later, being replaced by the half of C Company from F Company's left. Three sections of E Company, then in local reserve took over the duty of watching the left flank, and about 2100 hours a company of the 14th Sikhs came up to act as local reserve.

At 0200 hours on the 12th, the enemy opened heavy fire along the whole front. This died down about 0330 hours without anything untoward happening in our sector.

At 0630 hours, the half of C Company who were watching the ravine was withdrawn, as they were not required by day. With them returned Subedar-Major Sunder Singh, who had been wounded by shrapnel the night before, and, although in great pain, had refused to leave his post until they were ordered to withdraw. The shrapnel bullet was still in his knee when he returned.

During the morning, instructions were received to support by fire an advance to be made by the 6th Gurkhas on the left. The advance was timed for 1830 hours that evening. During the afternoon, the two machine guns of the 69th Punjabis, which were in position in 'F' Company's trench, were relieved by two guns belonging to the Armoured Motor Company, attached to the Naval Division; and a third gun of the same corps, previously with the New Zealanders on the right, moved down the trench to the left of No.4 Double Company. The remaining half of C Company now arrived and relieved E Company on the left of F Company. According to orders received in the morning, precisely at 1830 hours, rapid fire was opened on the Turkish trenches.

As the orders were to continue rapid fire until told to stop, a system of reliefs had to be arranged; because, in less than five minutes, some of the rifles were so hot that the men could not hold them. However, at 1845 hours, orders were received to continue with occasional rapid bursts only, as long as superiority of fire had been established. At 2300 hours, this was discontinued altogether, as news was received that the advance by the Gurkhas had been completely successful. Two double companies had occupied a commanding position to F Company's left front, overlooking the sea on one side, and slightly enfilading the Turkish front line on the other. This position was named Gurkha Bluff.

The next morning, when things became visible, another company of the Gurkhas moved up on the left of F Company, to link up the line with the position on Gurkha Bluff. The Turks, thinking we

Rough Sketch of Trenches Held by 89th Punjabis Gallipoli 8th – 13th May 1915

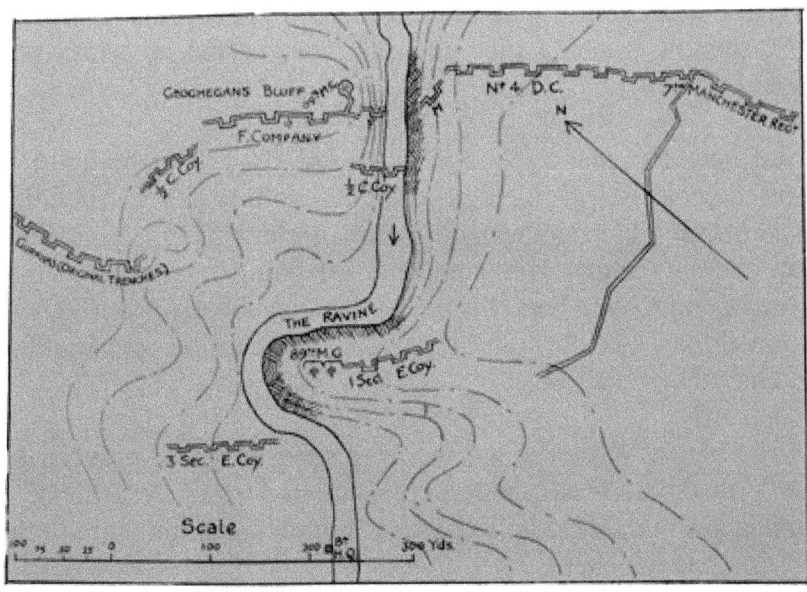

were attacking, got out of their trenches and were caught "on the hop " by fire from F Company and No.4 Double Company.

Another point was scored soon after. An observer in F Company trench noticed a thin wisp of steam rising out from the heathery scrub on the opposite slope. The spot was carefully marked down, and a machine gun laid carefully on it. On the gun opening fire, two Turkish gunners rose up and bolted from the post. Our rifles and the remaining gun immediately took up the target, with the result that gun and gunners were immediately knocked out we had no further trouble from snipers that day. Later in the morning, No 4 Double Company and some of the Manchester's on the right, to improve their field of fire, advanced about 100 yards and dug themselves in. This advance was rather costly. Many casualties occurred including Captain Scruby, who was severely wounded, but none could be brought in until after dark.

No.1528 Havildar Harnam Singh, who had taken the place of his

Indian officer, wounded during this advance, distinguished himself by his coolness and gallantry throughout this very trying day. Amongst the things, he, and No.1793 Sepoy Indar Singh, rendered first aid to Captain Scruby and brought him under cover of a shallow trench which the survivors of the advance were hastily constructing.

It was here, too, that Captain Scruby's orderly, Ramkishore Singh, showed great bravery and devotion by going back to Battalion Headquarters three times under heavy fire at close range to fetch water for his sahib. Unfortunately, on going forward the third time, he must have been hit, as he was never seen again. It was impossible to look for him by day, and stretcher-bearers failed to find him that night.

At 1800 hours that evening, we were relieved in the trenches by the 14th Sikhs, and the whole Battalion (less A B and D Companies, who were still at Stone Bridge) spent the night in the old first line trenches.

Next day May 14th, the Battalion moved a little farther back into bivouacs. That evening, orders were received to be ready to re-embark and return to Egypt. Apparently, it was not, at the time, considered desirable to have any Muhammedan troops on the Peninsula.

On the 15th leaving behind Captain Strong, Captain Engledue, Lieutenant Masters, and Second Lieutenant Hasluck to be attached to the 14th Sikhs, the Battalion wended it's in small parties (so as not to attract attention) to the beach. By midnight, we had embarked: Battalion Headquarters and personnel on H.T. *Suffolk*, and Regimental Transport on H. T. *Hymethis*. Both ships arrived in Alexandria on the 18th. During the short period the battalion spent on the peninsula, the battle casualties amounted in all to 2 British Officers, 5 Indian Officers, and over 100 other ranks killed, wounded or missing. This in spite of the fact that A, B and D Companies had not been employed in any actual fighting.

Chapter V

FRANCE JUNE TO DECEMBER 1915

From May 18th to the 22nd, the Battalion remained on board the Suffolk, under orders to proceed to Marseilles as soon as the necessary arrangements could be made (see Appendix III). Meanwhile, the regimental dump, which had been left behind at Port Said, rejoined.

On May 23rd the Battalion disembarked from the Suffolk, arid re-embarked on H.T. *Star of India*. The next morning we sailed for Marseilles, where we arrived on the afternoon of May 29th. Immediately after arrival, F Company, under Major Geoghegan, and a party of 20 rank and file under Captain Wood, landed and drew European clothing and equipment. Next morning, the remainder of the Battalion followed suit, while Major Geoghegan's party marched to Borelly racecourse, to pitch camp for the Battalion, and Captain Wood and his party entrained for the north, to take over equipment left behind by the 9th Bhopals .

The Battalion remained in camp for two nights. On June 1st, Captain E. J. Burdett, 11th Rajputs (attached to 9th Bhopals), joined us as No.4 Double Company Commander. This officer had only just corn away from the front line, and was expecting to go to Egypt with the 9th Bhopals It is most regrettable to have to relate that he was the first British office casualty sustained by the

Battalion in France, being killed near Port Arthur on June 25th.

The Battalion entrained at Prado Station on June 1st, arriving at Lestrem on the 4th. The same afternoon, after a short march, we found our advance party, who had arranged billets for us all in the village of Croix Marmeuse. Here Captain R. F. D. Burnett, 42nd Deoli Regiment and Lieutenant H. H. Greene, I.A.R.O., joined the Battalion for duty, and Private Tavard, 42nd French Territorial Regiment, late Professor in French literature at some American university, was attached to us as interpreter.

The Battalion remained in these billets until June 12th. We now, found ourselves in the place of the 9th Bhopals in the Ferozepore Brigade which consisted of the Connaught Rangers the 1st/4th London Regin1en the 129th Baluchis, and the 57th Rifles. Amongst other things taken over by the advance party were the G.S. wagons and limbers comprising the regimental transport, with a number of British personnel. This nucleus of 1 non-commissioned officer and 10 Army Service Corps drivers was not sufficient for all the transport, so that a number of sepoys had to be trained immediately in riding and driving. Instruction was also carried out in the fuzing and handling bombs, and in the use of respirators.

On June 6th, we were inspected by our Brigade Commander, Brigadier-General Egerton, and on the following day by Major-General H. d'U. Keary, Commanding Lahore Division, and on the 8th by Lieutenant-General Sir James Willcocks, commanding the Indian Corps.

On June 12th, the Ferozepore Brigade relieved the Jullundur Brigade in the trenches. In the morning, the C.O., Adjutant, and Double-Company Commanders went up to inspect the trenches to be taken over, and to arrange details of relief. At 1900 hours, the Battalion marched out of billets, leaving a depot of 1 Indian officer, 58 rank and file, 32 followers, 6 drabies, 11 British Army Service Corps personnel, and the interpreter under the Quartermaster, Lieutenant Rohde, Riez Bailleul. The second line train moved to Caloune-sur-Lys, where it remained under a guard of seven rank and file. At 2300 hours, guides were picked up at

Pont Logy. These led us to the front line trenches between Oxford Street and the La Bassée Road, which we took over from the 4th Suffolk Regiment. The relief was complete by 0200 hours. It was rather a coincidence that, during the relief, the machine gun officers of the two battalions should recognise each other by their voices. They had both been at the same school in the wilds of Perthshire, and had last seen each other five years before.

On the morning of the 13th, the Brigade Commander visited us in the trenches. This, our first day in the trenches, was a comparatively quiet one. In the evening, the usual routine was taken up, parties going back to take over rations that had been cooked during the day at the depot, and brought up to Pont Logy after dark. Patrols went out to gather information and counteract enemy patrolling. certain amount of cleaning up and other work could be done behind the line by day, but most of the digging anywhere in the forward area had to be done by night. During these first few days, parties went out nightly to improve our wire entanglements and to construct advanced posts for listening or other purposes. The first non-commissioned officer to show his worth was a Brahmin, Naik Ramji Misr (afterwards Jemadar), who night after night volunteered for patrol work, and on two occasions brought back very valuable information.

On the 13th, Captain James and our first reinforcements of 78 rank and file arrived in the billets we had just vacated. They had also brought along with them Second Lieutenant Peto, who had been left behind in Egypt sick. This party remained in billets for five days before being allowed to join the Battalion.

On June 15th, the Sirhind Brigade on our right carried out a minor operation with a view to sizing a portion of the German line. The Battalion remained in readiness to conform to the situation from 1700 hours onwards, but owing to the failure of the operation, no action on our part was necessary. Normal dispositions were resumed at 2017 hours. On June I6th and again on the 17th, as enemy snipers were causing casualties in our trenches, No.2254 Havildar Chiragh Din showed great pluck in going out in front of our line and, in broad daylight, locating and silencing the snipers on each occasion. After this, the art of sniping was practised.

Steadily in the Battalion, although it was, up till then, a subject about which we knew very little. On the 18th, the enemy shelled and destroyed the gunner observation post in the Battalion area. The same day, the enemy trenches were reported to be unusually full of men. However, as nothing came of it, it was surmised that reliefs must have been taking place. On the 19th, the G.O.C. Lahore Division congratulated the Battalion on the excellent work done during the past six days. A great deal of labour had been expended on improving defences and communications, counter-sniping work had been most successful, and a considerable amount of useful information had been supplied to higher authority. On the night of the 19th/20th, the Battalion was relieved by the 129th Baluchis and 57th Rifles, and moved into Brigade reserve in Loretto Road. The machine guns, with fifty rifles of 'E' Company, remained in the trenches as garrison of Port Arthur Keep, and No.4 Double Company in local reserve near Pont Logy. Captain James's draft was now absorbed into companies, while he himself took over the duty of Machine Gun Officer from Lieutenant Campbell at Port Arthur. It was in front of this redoubt, on the night of June 21st/22nd, that a party of E Company were improving the entanglement when they were heavily shelled by the enemy. Carrying out the orders of the British officer in charge, they withdrew under cover until the shelling died down. On arrival under cover Colour-Havildar Hira Tiwari, noticing that the British officer was not there, showed great devotion by going out again, in spite of the heavy fire, to look for him. Luckily, both of them returned unscathed.

On the 23rd, No.2 Double Company moved up in relief of No.4 Double Company, which, in turn, moved up to the firing line and support trenches, relieving the 129th Baluchis. On the 25th, the remainder of the Battalion moved in relieving the Connaught Rangers. It was on this night that Captain Burdett was killed, being shot through the head whilst observing over the parapet. The battalion held this portion of the trenches until June 28th. Work was the usual routine. During the period, No.2129 Havildar Kishun Singh and No.2352 Naik Muhammed Sadiq were both brought to notice, not only for volunteering over and over again for night patrol work, but also for the clear and valuable reports brought back by them.

On the night of June 28th/29th, being relieved by 1st/1st Gurkhas, the Battalion moved back into billets at Bout Deville, where we found the depot already settled in. During the first period of sixteen days in the trenches, our casualties were: British officers, killed 1; Indian officers, wounded 1, sick 2; other ranks, killed 3, wounded 69, sick 5.

The Battalion remained in these billets until July 6th. Three hours were taken up daily with parades and instruction, chiefly in bombing. And each night, working parties of at least 100 rank and file, under a British officer, were supplied for the construction of trench-works north of Neuve Chapelle: also, much to the joy of British officers, one week's leave to the United Kingdom was opened to them.

On July 1st, the machine guns of the five units were brigaded under Captain James, so that we lost the immediate services of this officer until the Indian Corps finally withdrew from the trenches. Lieutenant Greene was put in charge of the Battalion's Machine Gun Section in Captain James's place.

On July 5th, the Commanding Officer and Company Commanders inspected the trenches in front of Neuve Chapelle. The next evening, the Battalion moved in, relieving the 40th Pathans and the 47th Sikhs. The arrangements for this relief were excellent. The relief was complete by 2300 hours, which proved to be an unusually early hour for this time of the year. The depot, on this occasion, was located in billets south of La Gorgue. The Battalion, together with the 1/4th London Regiment, was now holding a sub-section of the line, which included the Duck's Bill and the trenches to the north-east for several hundred yards. This period in the trenches was marked chiefly by enemy artillery activity, various points in our trench system, more especially the Duck's Bill and the Duck's Neck, being shelled daily. This necessitated heavy repair work every night.

On July 8th, Major Geoghegan was wounded in the head a few minutes before he was due to leave the trenches en route for a week's leave in England. The wound, however, was not too serious; so that, after treatment at the regimental aid post and later at a field ambulance near the rail way station, Major Geoghegan was able to take advantage of his leave.

On July 10th, the Sirhind Brigade, on our right, reported that the enemy wire on their front had been cut. This report, combined with unusual artillery activity against our own wire and front line system, raised suspicions of an intended enemy attack. The Battalion, therefore, remained in constant readiness throughout the next two nights, sending out special patrols each night. The patrols had nothing unusual to report, and in the end, as no attack developed, things became normal again.

On July 14th, the Battalion was relieved by the 2nd Bn. The Black Watch. Unfortunately, it started raining early in the afternoon, and continued to do so until 0200 hours the next morning. Trenches and the surrounding country were a sea of mud, in consequence of which the relief was carried out with considerable difficulty and was not complete until 0330 hours. Daylight found some of us still struggling to get away from the trenches.

The casualties for this period in the trenches (July 6th to 15th) were: British officers, wounded 1; other ranks, killed 2, wounded 21, sick 8.

By 0530 hours on the 15th, we were all settled in billets in Pont-du-Hem and Bout Deville. The same evening, we marched, via Lestrem and Merville, to new billets in Arrewage and Caudescure, where we arrived about 2300 hours. Here we were told that we were going to have three weeks "rest"! After four days spent in smartening-up drills and route marches, training in grenades, and so on, we had to change billets once more. On the 21st, the Battalion marched to Haverskerque, where these new billets were to be. Our march led us through the very fine Forêt de Nieppe. At Haverskerque, Second Lieutenant K. W. R. O'Reilly, with a draft of I Indian officer and 57 other ranks, joined the Battalion, and Jemadar Bakshish Singh and one man rejoined from the Indian Hospital in Egypt. On July 27th, the new drafts were inspected by Sir James Willcocks.

On this day also, Lieutenant Campbell took over the duties of Quarter Master from Lieutenant Rohde, who had to undergo an operation in England. On his return to the Battalion in September, Lieutenant Rohde was appointed company officer, and served with his company until he was killed in Mesopotamia in April, 1916.

On the 29th, the Battalion marched to La Gorgue. Lieutenant-Colonel Murray now took over command of the Battalion for a few days, during the absence of Lieutenant-Colonel Campbell, who was temporarily commanding the Brigade.

On the 30th, a working party was supplied to the Royal Engineers, and the Commanding Officer and Company Commanders visited the trenches. The next day (July 31st), the Battalion marched to new billets in the Rue du Ponch, and the same evening relieved the 2nd Bn. Seaforth Highlanders and the 46th Sikhs in the trenches between Oxford Street and Church Street. These trenches we held until August 9th. During this period, the Boche was comparatively quiet by day. Both sides, however, were very busy by night, endeavouring to improve their own wire and construct advanced posts. This led to considerable patrol activity, followed by endeavours on each side to "strafe" the other's working parties. No.3 Double Company were in the front line, their portion including The Neb. Immediately after taking over, a patrol from that company drove off an enemy patrol with bombs, and for the next four nights No.1766 Havildar Jagdeo Dube (afterwards Jemadar) showed great gallantry in going out with a grenade party and forcing the enemy to abandon his sap-head opposite The Neb. On the 3rd, a patrol of E Company and another of F, both brought in good information concerning this sap.

On the 5th, the enemy displayed a notice, Warschaw Gefallen, and at 1500 hours sent up a rocket, which was followed by cheering. The same evening, No.4 Double Company relieved No.3 in the front line. For the next three nights, large parties were out in 'No Man's Land' wiring or furnishing covering parties for working parties along our own front and that of the Connaught

Rangers. For the first two nights, we worked unmolested, but on the night of the 7th/8th the enemy opened up with machine gun fire. The working parties and part of the covering party were withdrawn. The remainder of the covering party (from No.4 Double Company) remained in position, to cover the removal of casualties. On this occasion, Captain Burnett and his orderly, Udham Singh, Naik Mohd, Sadiq (now Subedar), No.1684

Lance-Naik Chanda Singh, No.2090 Sepoy Nur Dad, and No.1545 Sepoy Mohd Khan were brought to notice for gallantry in bringing in three wounded men who had to be lifted over our own wire under machine-gun fire. The last man was brought in in daylight.

As some doubts were cast on the accuracy of our patrol reports and the positions they reached during their nightly prowlings, a novel method of verifying their reports was used. Each patrol was furnished with a small flag which was planted at the farthest point reached. As daylight broke, these flags could be picked up through binoculars or with the naked eye, This enabled officers to be certain of the correctness of reports, and helped them to locate accurately various items reported.

On the night of the 8th/9th, it was possible to locate pretty accurately a new enemy trench by this system. On this night, four patrols each brought back good information. One commanded by Subedar Gulab Khan, another by Naik Harnam Singh (this patrol planted their flag a few yards from the German front line); the third patrol merely confirmed the reports of the first two, and the fourth patrol, composed of three signallers, No.2334 Lance-Naik Nur Hussein, No.2570 Lance-Naik Ali Gaur Khan and No.2530 Sepoy Chanan Khan, brought back a great amount of detailed information that was most useful.

That same night, by way of retaliation for the night before, No.4 Double Company sent out a party which again bombed the enemy out of their saphead opposite The Neb.

The next evening, we were relieved by the 57th Rifles, and moved into Brigade reserve at Loretto Road.

FRANCE, 1915.

1. ROUGE CROIX CROSS ROADS. 2. OXFORD STREET, NEAR NEUVE CHAPELLE. 3. AID POST DUG-OUTS, EDGWARE ROAD.

Nothing could be done here all day ' as the area was a favourite target for enemy shell fire. Enemy aircraft were also increasingly active at this period. Certain officers and non-commissioned officers made daylight journeys into Bethune for special instruction in the new bomb, the Mills hand grenade, and working parties went out nightly, digging and carrying in the Neuve Chapelle area.

At 2130 hours on the 16th, the battalion, having been relieved by the 4th Kings Liverpool Regiment, marched to "rest" billets at La Croix Marmeuse and Zelobes.

The casualties during this period (July 31st to August 16th) were: Other ranks, killed, 2, wounded, 21.

On August 17th, the Battalion was further reinforced by the arrival of Captain Davson, 2 Indian officers, and 98 other ranks, all from the 82nd Punjabis; and, later in the day, Lieutenant Bampfield, 90th Punjabis (attached to 15th Sikhs), joined for duty. These reinforcements brought the strength of the Battalion up to 13 British officers, 20 Indian officers, and 720 Indian other ranks.

While in these billets, the men had their first experience of hot baths behind the line, a bathing station at Port Riqueul being available for them.

It was during this period of "rest" that a working party was sent to the help of a French farmer near Rouge Croix to assist in the harvesting of his crops. This old gentleman had experienced some difficulty the day before in teaching men of a London regiment how to use the French hand-sickle. Great amusement arose when he started to teach the Punjabis. He was requested to stand aside and not interfere. His surprise turned to cries of delight when he saw the Indians settle down to their job. It was not long before they had the large field cut and arranged neatly in stooks.

On August 20th, C Company marched up to the forward area to provide a garrison for Richebourg Post, near Richebourg St.

Vaast, and guards for four other posts nearby. The same day, a party of snipers proceeded to Aire to test the telescopic-sighted rifles on regimental charge.

On the 23rd, Capt Davson's draft was inspected by the Indian Corps Commander.

On the evening of the next day, August 24th, the Battalion moved up to La Couture, in Brigade reserve. With the exception of two days spent marching behind the line, the Battalion was not to see "rest" billets again for sixty-four days.

Owing to its being constantly the target for enemy shell fire, La Couture was practically uninhabited, and we found that, to avoid attention from the enemy, and to keep ourselves "up to the mark", daily parades had to be confined to P.T. and short runs after dusk. The depot was accommodated in a farm close to La Couture.

About this time, new gas-masks with rube mouth-pieces and glass eye-pieces were issued to the unit, and practice was carried out with them. On arrival in France, we had been supplied with the original face-pad, which was fitted over mouth and nostrils; this was later replaced with a bag, with talc eye-pieces, which went over the head, the edges being tucked inside one's coat collar. The next issue was of the new mask, mentioned above, which was an improvement on the gas-helmet with talc eye-pieces.

On the 26th orders were received to relieve the 2nd Warwickshire regiment and the South Staffordshire Regiment in the line. The usual party went up to visit the trenches beforehand, and at 1845 hours on the 27th the Battalion marched from La Couture. The relief was completed, in almost record time, by 2125 hours. We found ourselves holding a portion of the line in front of Rue du Bois, which included the Boar's Head (otherwise known as the Glory Hole). Our left was just exclusive of Bond Street, and our right extended a little further to the right of the Boar's Head. The Boar's Head was situated in a former German trench which had been double blocked. He most advanced post in this trench was within twenty yards of a similar post of the enemy.

For the first two days the enemy in this section gave us little trouble. Our communication trenches were found to be dangerous by day, as they were not properly defiladed. The enemy had the range accurately to all exposed spots . This matter was soon put right. More shells being now available our artillery began really to worry the German front line. This goaded the Boche to retaliate. On the 29th, he started on the troops on our immediate left, and
on the 30th he turned his attention to the 89th, putting over a large number of rifle grenades, and causing some casualties in our front line.

On the night of August 31st/1st September, we took heavy toll of an enemy working party opposite the Boar's Head, causing them to cease work for the night.

Our patrols in this section had complete ascendency over the enemy by night, reconnoitring right up to his wire, which, in places, was only twenty feet from his parapet, driving back all enemy patrols whenever met with, and frequently causing the enemy to evacuate his listening posts. The men had developed a taste for bombing, and seemed to revel in it

Just before dark on September 1st, Captain Wood, in charge of the regimental snipers, had scored a visible hit. As the man fell, several of the enemy snipers exposed themselves to clear view. Rapid fire was immediately opened on them, with good effect.

Later on, the same night, a patrol of three Sikhs, under No.1654 Havildar Harnan Singh, while on patrol came across an enemy listening post containing fifteen of the enemy. This gallant little patrol observing their orders that the enemy were to be harried as much as possible, at once attacked and bombed the enemy. On being counter-attacked by the enemy, the patrol again bombed them, and finally drove them back with rapid fire. In this episode, No.2081 Sepoy Sawaya Singh (90th Punjabis) specially distinguished himself. This patrol was warmly congratulated by the Brigade Commander the next day.

After this, the enemy tried the effect of constant bursts of

machine gun fire at regular intervals, with a view to harassing our working parties and repelling our patrols. This, however, enabled us to locate definitely several of his guns; and, as his own patrols were
not out during these periods of gun activity, our patrols, by a combination of running, crawling and lying still, were able to get right up to the enemy wire, and make a complete reconnaissance of it.

The establishment of three *minenwerfers*, one large and two small, in the enemy line now gave rise to several "hates", in which we eventually got the upper hand. In this, Second Lieutenant O'Reilly and his band of merry men played a prominent part with a West spring gun. During these "hates" the Boar's Head was twice blown to bits, which caused a lot of extra repair work to be done at night. Luckily, on each occasion the garrison of the post had just withdrawn behind the second parapet after carrying out a "hate" on the German salient.

On the night of September 4th/5th, No.1528 Havildar Harnan Singh, who bad previously distinguished himself in Gallipoli, again showed great pluck in carrying out a successful and dangerous reconnaissance of a new enemy trench to the left of the Boar's Head. During the whole time, he was under machine gun and rifle fire, and at one time a number of the enemy came out of their trench to endeavour to capture him. He managed, however, to evade them, and return with most valuable information.

On September 9th, the Battalion was relieved by the 57th Rifles, and moved back into Brigade reserve near Richebourg St. Vaast, finding garrisons for nine strong points near the Rue du Bois. This relief ,vas carried out during the day-time. The enemy evidently had some inkling of what was happening, and started to "strafe" us with their *minenwerfer*. Thinking that this should not be allowed, No.1816 Havildar Sheorattan Singh and No.2079 Sepoy Sirinewas Misr, without asking permission, crawled out towards the German trenches, in broad daylight, and silenced one of the smaller guns with hand grenades!

Back in Richebourg St Vaast, the Battalion paraded by day under cover of the trees and houses, and every night had to furnish working parties for digging or for carrying stores.

On September 23rd, the Battalion took over the front line trenches again from the 57th Rifles. We felt like lambs being led to the slaughter, as the Battle of Loos was looming up in the near future. However, we were all hoping for an advance, and the time had con1e at last, when Kitchener's New Army were to receive their baptism of fire.

On the 24th, Lieutenant-Colonel Campbell was withdrawn from the Battalion as a reserve Brigade Commander, and a new toy, in the shape of smoke bombs, was distributed along the front line. All day on the 24th our artillery had been bombarding the German lines. and even all night the thunder of guns was incessant. At 0430 hours, the Battalion stood to arms, and at 0556 hours, smoke bombs were ignited and thrown out in front of the trenches, with the object of creating a smoke cloud to disguise the entire front. The wind, which was contrary to the alignment of the particular portion of trenches held by the Battalion, blew the smoke back across our own front line every now and then. However, a fairly respectable screen was maintained by throwing the bombs well out into "No Man's Land". At the same time, rifle and machine gun fire was opened up. Our orders were to advance if the enemy vacated their front line. Objectives were allotted to the different platoons and companies. Two platoons of No.3 Double Company were given the honour of capturing the Ferme du Bois. This ruined farmhouse in front of the right of our portion of the line had been converted into a very strong redoubt capable, probably, of withstanding the onslaught of a whole battalion. At 0730 hours, patrols went out to find out if the Boche were still in occupation of their trenches. By 0805 hours, we got information that they were still there.

Soon after 0800 hours, we received orders to be prepared to advance, as it was rumoured that an attack by the Meerut Division in front of Neuve Chapelle had been successful. This order seemed unnecessary, as we had been standing to arms since 0430 hours. However, to confirm the reports of our patrols, Jemadar Bagga Singh, taking with him a field telephone, went out at 1100 hours, and lay up under the enemy's wire all day till 1900 hours, sending back valuable information on several occasions, not only as to the presence of the enemy, but of their movements, the state of their wire, and positions of machine gun emplacements. He was exposed the whole time not only to the enemy's fire, but to the fire of our own artillery. This Indian officer, with utter disregard for his personal safety, performed another reconnaissance at daylight the next day, confirming information collected the day before.

During the night of September 25th/26th, our patrols were out in force, and had more or Jess complete command of "No Man's Land". The patrols went out with the idea, if possible, of cutting the enemy's wire and preventing him from mending what damage had already been done. No.2173 Sepoy Rukham Din (82nd Punjabis) and No.2120 Sepoy Muhammed Khan, two members of one patrol, having crept up close to the German trenches, threw several grenades into their front line, although under a sustained fire. The former was then severely wounded in the shoulder, but carried on with his patrol duty until overcome by faintness. Sepoy Muhammed Khan had already shown the stuff he was made of on a previous occasion when on night patrol with a non-commissioned officer. The non-commissioned officer had been badly wounded, and, to allow him to get back unmolested, this sepoy crawled up to the enemy wire and placed his head-dress on a stake, thus drawing their fire. No.2146 Lance-Naik Gauhar Din, in charge of another patrol on the night of the 25th/26th, also crept up to the German trenches, and threw five grenades into the front line.

Another patrol on this night with an Indian officer in charge got rather badly knocked about. While examining the enemy wire, they were detected. Fire was opened on them, wounding the Indian officer and two of the patrol (four other ranks). The Boche followed up by sending a party to finish them off. No.3275 Naik Suleiman (91st Punjabis), one of the patrol, turned on the enemy single-handed and drove them back with grenades. He undoubtedly saved the patrol by his gallant action, which left them free to withdraw with the three wounded men.

On the 26th, as operations at Loos were at a standstill, our attitude was relaxed, and we returned more or less to normal trench warfare again That night, our patrols were again active, cutting the enemy wire. During intervals when our patrols were not out, our machine guns opened fire prevent the enemy from repairing damage done to their wire. September 27th passed uneventfully, but that night, when our patrols went out the found the enemy endeavouring to repair their wire. The first patrol get into touch with the enemy was one commanded by No.1998 Naik Narain Singh. Without considering the numbers against them, this gallant little patrol at once bombed them, causing the enemy to scuttle back in their trenches. Not content with this, Naik Narain Singh and his patrol of three men advanced and tried to cut the wire, but were foiled in the attempt by heavy rifle fire which the enemy opened on them, wounding one of the patrol severely. The patrol withdrew, taking turns to carry the wounded comrade. Our machine guns opened bursts of fire whenever our patrols were not out.

On September 28th Lieutenant-Colonel Campbell resumed command of the Battalion. The enemy harassed us pretty well all day with *minenwerfer*, apparently in the hope of finding our machine guns, which had effectually kept his working parties tied to their trenches the night before. During the night, a patrol, commanded by No.163 Havildar Fateh Khan brought in valuable information regarding most of the enemy wire in our sector.

The next day, the *minenwerfer* redoubled their efforts, but did us no serious damage. That night, when our patrols went out, they were unable to get very far, as the enemy already had a strong covering force in position and a party just beginning work on their much battered wire. In accordance with previous instructions, however, our patrols all withdrew at once, and shortly afterwards a sudden burst of rifle and machine gun fire along the whole of our front drove the enemy back to their trenches from which they did not emerge for the rest of the night. They were so thoroughly rattled that they allowed a patrol of Rajputs, under No.1287 Havildar Baldeo Singh (later Jemadar) to take great liberties. This patrol finding an enemy listening post unoccupied, cut all the wire

round it and threw it into the trench. They then proceeded to fill in
the trench by pushing in the parapet on top of the dismantled wire. This they completed just as dawn was breaking. Before leaving, however, they shot at two Germans, and claimed to have killed one of them at least. The same night, another patrol cut four pathways through the enemy's already-damaged wire. During the next day, the enemy retaliated by shelling our supports and reserves, and subjecting our front line to a slight bombardment by trench mortars.

Thus ended September. Twice during the last week the Brigade Commander complimented the 89th on its good patrol work.

Hitherto, whilst our patrols were out, our machine guns had remained silent. The enemy now began to size this up; and whenever our guns ceased firing they pushed out their own patrols and their covering and working parties. So, on the night of October 1st/2nd, a patrol went out from the centre of our section, covered by fire from the flanking companies. This patrol succeeded in reaching the enemy wire and cutting portions of it without molestation. On the return of this patrol, a patrol was sent out from each flank, but without any covering fire. The enemy parties, recognising their cue, came out and started work on the repair of their wire. Our patrols at once returned to report; whereupon, along the whole front line, the Battalion opened fire with good results. The next night, we sent out no patrols whatever, but contented ourselves with frequent and irregular bursts of fire along the whole line.

The next day, October 3rd, the Battalion was relieved by the 8th South Staffordshires. In accordance with the usual routine, the machine guns were relieved by day. Our guns, having been relieved, were just leaving the front line when the Boche opened up a vigorous "hate" with rifle grenades, trench mortars, and field guns. Two parties laden with machine guns and tripods, etc., making their way along a narrow inspection trench, seeing a minenwerfer shell coming over, ran to try to dodge it. Most unfortunately, they ran towards each other and got jammed in the trench right in the path of the shell, which exploded. One man was killed, and Lieutenant Greene and several sepoys were wounded. Without any further mishap, the trenches were handed over to the incoming regiment, and the 89th marched back a long twelve miles to billets at Chapelle Duvelle, a small village halfway between Estaires and Merville. The last company marched in at 0330 hours.

The casualties for the period of forty-one days amounted to I British officer wounded, 1 Indian officer killed (Jemadar Jagdam Singh), and 2 wounded (Subedar Fakir Mohd. and Jemadar Kesar Shah); 8 other ranks killed, and 144 wounded, of whom many, unfortunately, died. Jemadar Jagdam Singh was a very popular Indian officer, and had been brought to notice several times for bravery in the field. He was the victim of a German sniper. Being shot through the head whilst trying to avoid a particularly muddy pool in one of the front line trenches.

Captain Conder, of the 112th Infantry, joined for duty on this day October 3rd. this officer only stayed with the battalion a short while, being transferred to the 1st/8th Gurkha Rifles nine days later as they were short of officers.

On the 4th it snowed, and the Battalion remained in their billets. The Brigade Commander paid a visit to the officers. In the evening, orders were received to move early the next day to new billets in Rue de Ponch. The next morning, whilst the Battalion was parading to march to the new area the Quartermaster set off on a bicycle, followed by bicycle orderlies from each company, to take over the billets. About four inches of snow was lying on the roads. The Quartermaster himself found it hard enough to cycle along without side-slipping, but had to stop every hundred yards or so to, wait for the orderlies, who afforded an amusing spectacle in their ungainly attempts to master their machines. The Battalion arrived at the new billets just twenty minutes after the Quartermaster and his little band of heroes. The next day, October 6th, one company was again obliged to move, as the farm it occupied was allotted to another area. It had scarcely finished moving in when the Commandant received orders that the Battalion was to be attached to the Jullundur Brigade, and to go back into the trenches that night.

This was due to an emergency readjustment of the line in other brigades. The 59th Rifles, then in Brigade reserve at Ludhiana Lodge, moved up into the front line, and the 89th took their place.

Before the Battalion moved up to the trenches, Lieutenant-Colonel Campbell received a letter from Brigadier-General Egerton congratulating the Battalion on what it had done during the last few weeks.

The Battalion was attached to the Jullundur Brigade from October 6th to 11th when the Brigade was relieved by the Ferozepore Brigade and we found ourselves back with our own Brigade. The Battalion remained the whole time at Ludhiana Lodge, where it found itself comfortably accommodated in dug-outs. Large working parties had to be furnished every night for digging or carrying stores. On October 11th when the Ferozepore

Brigade relieved the Jullundur Brigade, the Battalion supplied one company to garrison six redoubts. The remainder of the Battalion remained at Ludhiana Lodge.

On October 12th, Lieutenant-Colonel Murray and Lieutenant Bampfield were transferred to the 58th Rifles, and Second Lieutenant H. Humphrey I.A.R.O., joined the Battalion This officer, although figuring as a Second Lieutenant, w:as a man of mature age, with many years' experience as a volunteer in India. Had he been serving in the New Army, he would undoubtedly have held field rank. He put in much good work with the Battalion until severely wounded in Mesopotamia in March, 1916. Every endeavour was made to get him back to the 89th, but he was subsequently claimed for duty on the Embarkation Staff at Karachi, an appointment for which his previous civilian experience in that port rendered him eminently suitable.

On the 13th, a dummy attack, which was intended to draw the enemy's fire and make him expose himself, was carried out in the front line. At 1230 hours, a smoke cloud was formed in the front line, while our artillery and machine guns bombarded and searched the enemy's various trenches and works in accordance with a previously arranged plan. At 1345 hours, our artillery fanned a smoke barrage. At 1356 hours, our infantry in the front line opened rapid fire and made a pretence of going over the top, making use of dummy figures. Our artillery then dropped a bombardment on the enemy's front line trenches. All that the 89th had to do was to stand to arms the whole time. The enemy replied with 5.9s and field guns, but did no serious damage. During this show, we had three men wounded and one buried by the collapse of a dug-out, but he was able to pick himself out suffering only from shock. By 1430 hours, all was quiet again.

On the 13th, Captain Davson was transferred to the 58th Rifles, and Captain Martelli, Queen's Regiment, joined for duty. The Battalion remained in reserve at Ludhiana Lodge until October 19th. During this period, Subedar Fakir Mohammed was again wounded; this time, while in charge of a party carrying R.E. stores up to "No Man's Land".

On the 20th, the 89th took over the front line trenches near The Neb from the 57th Rifles. The relief was carried out during the afternoon by small parties at a time, and was complete by 1845 hours.

This portion of the line had been held by us before, in August. About midnight on the first night, one of our listening posts reported sounds of the enemy working with picks. We opened up with machine gun fire, which immediately drew rifle fire in reply, but with no effect.

We ourselves were rather busy preparing our own trenches for the winter so the next few nights were uneventful. Both the enemy and ourselves ere occupied every night, erecting wire entanglements and improving the trenches generally. Occasionally we used to break off to "strafe" each other's working parties.

On the night of October 22nd/23rd, our patrol went out with the idea of strafing enemy patrols, which had been particularly active the night before, but they encountered none. The next night,

Havildar Fateh Khan, who has previously been mentioned for good work, went out alone and lay up within forty yards of the enemy. He remained in observation of an enemy party, which was sent out, until a working party behind them had got well down to their work. He then returned to our front line and gave us certain information which enabled us to open a most effective fire on the enemy. On the night of the 24th/25th, our brigaded machine guns opened up a one-minute burst of fire on roads in rear of the enemy's line, where it was thought their ration parties used to collect. This fire must have been effective, because our support lines and the area from which the machine guns had been firing were heavily shelled next morning.

On the 26th, Second Lieutenants Bates and G. C. L. Wadley, both I.A.R.O., reported their arrival. The former officer unhappily was killed later in Mesopotamia near Rohde's Picquet in April, 1916. The latter served with the Battalion or at the Depot until 1922, when he was "axed", together with a number of other good officers of the Indian Army. On this same day, enemy aircraft were active, and one aeroplane, spotting for artillery, came over our lines, but was driven back by our machine gun fire.

On the 27th, the Battalion was relieved by the 59th Rifles. The relief was complete by 2040 hours, and we marched back to billets in La Gorgue.

 Casualties during this spell of seven days were 20 other ranks wounded of whom two subsequently died

This was the last period of trench warfare that the Battalion was to experience in France, and was the finish of that almost continuous spell of sixty-four days mentioned previously.

Many instances describing acts of devotion and bravery have been mentioned here and elsewhere, and it is thought that it would be fitting to remember here that little band of heroes that one never hears much about- namely, the regimental signallers. These men had to go out very often under heavy fire, to find and mend breaks
in the cables, and to keep communication at all times, regardless

of enemy action or weather, and often had to fight against sleep. It was greatly due to No.1585 Havildar Sakhi Mohammed (afterwards Jemadar) and to those non-commissioned officers who succeeded him later, that all through the war the signallers of the 89th earned out their duties in a most efficient manner.

For the next eleven days, the Battalion remained in La Gorgue. On October 31st, we first heard that the Lahore Division would shortly leave France. Draught horses were replaced by mules, and Army Service Corps personnel relieved by Indian drivers. British officers were given every opportunity for short leave to England. Several of us were able to enjoy two visits of seven days each during the period of waiting for orders for this final move by train to Marseilles.

On November 4th, Lieutenant-Colonel Campbell left us, much to the regret of all ranks, to take command of the 9th Brigade, but we all wished him the best of luck in his new command. The command of the Battalion now devolved on Major N. M. Geoghegan.

On November 8th, the Battalion marched from La Gorgue to billets well out of the fighting area, at Le Cornet Brassard, near Berguette. Here we remained until the 18th, when we moved to Glomenghem, a village three miles west of Aire. One day, whilst the 89th were at this place, detachments from all Indian units concentrated near Aire, where they were inspected by H.R.H. the Prince of Wales.

On the 29th, the Battalion moved to fresh billets at Lugyi, a few miles south-west of Glomengham, and on December 2nd we moved again to Febvin Palfart, about seven and a half miles west of Lillers.

Since leaving La Gorgue on November 8th, in each place that the Battalion was billeted the attitude of the inhabitants towards all ranks and the comfort, and sometimes luxury, of the billets was strikingly different from that experienced nearer the fighting area. So it was with a certain amount of reluctance that we received our

Map of France
Showing portion of front held by the Indian Corps
June – October 1915

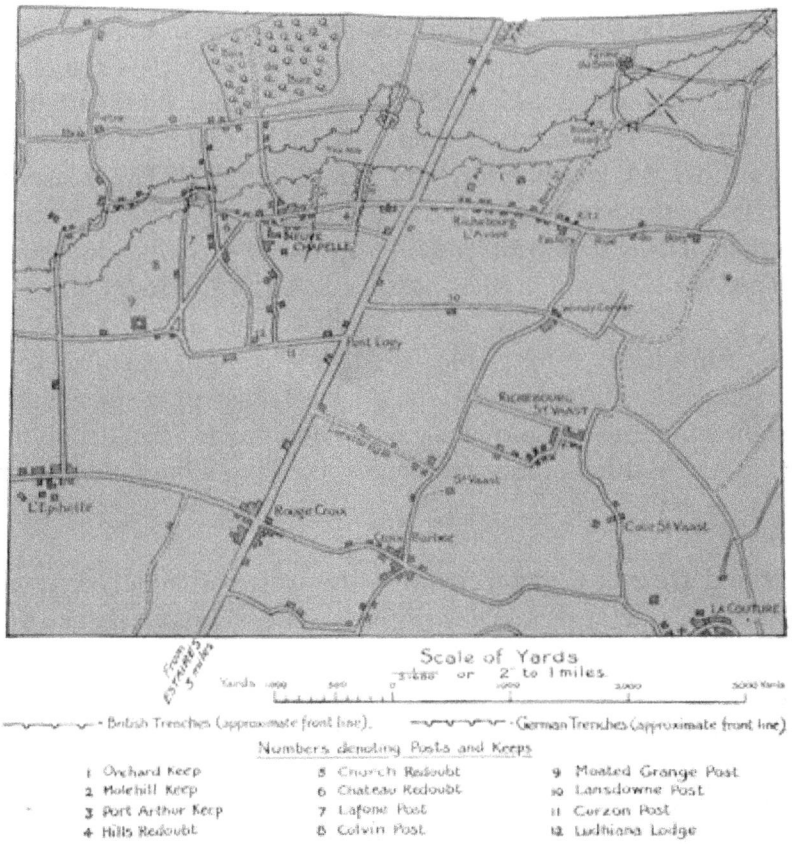

orders to entrain at Lillers for Marseilles on December 11th; however, as the destination of the Battalion was unknown, all ranks looked forward expectantly to new experiences.

On the evening of December 9th, a small party of sepoys and followers, under Lieutenant Campbell and Subedar-Major Sunder Singh Bahadur, marched to Lillers to cook food for the Battalion for the four days' train journey. This party arrived at Lillers Station late at night, in torrents of rain (which continued most of the night). When rations and fuel had been drawn, Lieutenant

Campbell confessed that the question of drying the soaking-wet fuel (mostly coal) and cooking the food was beyond his powers, and left the Subedar-Major to carry on. It says much for that gallant little party who, drenched to the skin themselves, sat down doggedly, dried up a swamp, made bunds to keep the water out, made shelters with their own water-proof capes, and by 0600 hours the next morning had completed their task. The Battalion marched into the station yard at 0730 hours, and entrained immediately. The transport, under Second Lieutenant O'Reilly, was left behind, and did not entrain until next day. The transport was destined never to rejoin us, and it was only with difficulty that S con? - Lieutenant O'Reilly and a few of the personnel rejoined the Battalion in Mesopotamia in March, 1916.

The 89th arrived at Marseilles at 2100 hours on December 13th and detrained and marched to the docks. Transport carts, without draught animals, were provided, and had to be man-handled to the docks. At 2300 hours the same night, the battalion embarked on H.T. *Canada.*

On board we met Captain Scruby, who was then attached to the M.L.O.'s office at Marseilles. Reinforcement, in the shape of a draft of 96 rank and file, embarked with the Battalion.

The next morning, the Canada, with the 59th Rifles, and ourselves on board, sailed on a zigzag course for Alexandria. This port was reached on the afternoon of December 19th. According to instructions received here, we proceeded at once for Port Said and Basra

Chapter VI

MESOPOTAMIA JANUARY TO AUGUST 1916

On January 1st, 1916, the Canada, then in the Persian Gulf, received orders to call at Koweit; this place was reached the next afternoon. As the Canada was of too deep a draught to cross the bar at the mouth of the Shatt-el-Arab, the B.I. steamer *Nizam* came alongside, and the two battalions were transferred to that ship early on the 3rd.

Basra was reached at 1500 hours on January 4th, but, no barges being available for disembarkation, we had to remain on board until the morning of the 6th. When disembarkation was complete, the Battalion, together with the 59th Rifles, marched into camp at Makina Masus. Here we spent the next day re-equipping and fitting out all ranks with khaki drill. Captain Chapman, with Jemadar Indar Singh and 76 other ranks as reinforcements joined here.

The Battalion was now almost up to strength. The British officers who had come from France were: Lieutenant-Colonel Geoghegan, as Commandant; Captain Wood, Captain Burnett, M.C., Captain James, and Lieutenant Rohde, as Company Commanders; Captain Crawford, as Adjutant; and Lieutenant Campbell, as Quartermaster; Lieutenants Humphrey, Peto, and Wadley, as company officers, and Lieutenant Bates, in charge of

Colonel N. M. GEOGHEGAN, D.S.O.

the Machine Gun Section. Lieutenant Sondhi was attached to the Battalion as Medical Officer just before leaving France.

On January 8th, the 59th Rifles and ourselves, together with a medical unit, were formed into the "3rd Echelon", and marched to Gurmat Ali (2½ miles), with orders to join General Aylmer's force at Ali Gharbi. The word "echelon" was commonly used to denote any mixed body of troops moving about behind the line, and may have varied from thirty or so details rejoining their units to two or more battalions.

The transport allotted to the Battalion was composed of 130 mules

and 3 mahelas (boats capable of carrying about forty tons). Rations for one month for the men and for four and a half days for the animals were loaded on one mahela, men's kit on another, and tents on the third. The ration mahela was the only one to arrive at Gurmat Ali that night, as some hitch occurred at the loading jetty in Basra. The Battalion camped that night without any bedding, and only British officers had tents. To complete our discomfort, it rained hard all night.

Next day (the 9th), the echelon marched thirteen miles to Nahr Umr. Owing to the rain, the ground was wet and muddy, and the going was very heavy, but the number of stragglers (two) was very small, considering that the troops had only just disembarked after a long sea voyage. At Nahr Umr, one of the missing mahelas turned up, but the men were still without their kits. Orders were received here to wait for the missing mahela so, the next day, being fine, was spent in drying clothes and cleaning up. On the 11th, owing to the shortage of rations for the mules, the echelon continued its march, and arrived at Shafi (12½ miles). Here we received news of the missing mahela having arrived at Gurmat Ali with only a portion of its crew. So, on the 12th, Lieutenant Rohde and twenty-five men were left behind to help, while the remainder of the echelon marched to Kurna (14 miles). Here more rations were drawn for the mules. Early on the 13th, the missing mahela joined us, and continued with us on our march the same day to Sakricha Canal (11½ miles). The remainder of the march to Amara was completed in six days. Halts were made at Ezra's Tomb (12 miles), Abu Rubah (11 miles), Qalat Salih (11 miles), and Abu Sidrah (12 miles).

From Basra to Qalat Salih, the route led us along the right bank of the Tigris, but the river was crossed by a pontoon bridge at a point about two miles north of this latter place, and the remainder of our march was continued along the left bank. The going was still very bad; often the column had to wade ankle-deep in water, and at the best the ground was like a wet ploughed field.

The O.C. Echelon decided to call a day's halt at Abu Sidrah, but, as the camping ground was small and the next march, to Amara, was twenty- one miles, Colonel Geoghegan pushed on the next day to another camping ground six miles farther on. On the 19th, the Battalion, on the arrival of the remainder of the echelon, marched from this camp to Amara. Here the echelon halted for one day. Rations and pay were drawn, and clothing and equipment dried.

On the 21st, the echelon set out to march to Fudayim Ruins (12 miles). Soon after starting, heavy rain fell, accompanied by an extremely cold east wind. All were soaked to the skin, and the going was heavier than ever. Considerable difficulty was experienced in getting the mules through the flooded irrigation canals. Finally, about two miles short of Fudayim, the Tigris was found to have burst its banks. This successfully cut us off from our objective. The echelon therefore pitched camp on the highest available piece of ground, and hurriedly constructed a bund three feet high all round, to prevent the camp from being flooded. Several men were knocked out from exposure to the wet and cold.

The next day, neighbouring Arabs, who had quickly assembled to save their crops from the flood, had managed to reduce the gap in the river bank to one of six feet, by making mattresses of the local thorny bush and gradually closing the gap with these weighted down with clods of earth. By noon on the 23rd, the gap was finally closed, and the echelon crossed in sing]e file.Although all mule loads were carried by the mahelas, the mules only marched, with great difficulty over the swampy ground, often sinking nearly up to their g1rths. After a march of two and a half miles the echelon had to halt again, as the mules were unable to go farther.

The next day, we were able to cover eight miles to Wail Shujah. Five miles farther on at Kumait, the river had again burst its banks, and here, on the following day we caught up the echelon in front of us. Mule rations were now running short so one of the mahelas was emptied, and Lieutenant Campbell with a small escort was sent back to Amara to draw more. On the 27th, the echelon was able to continue its march, but could only cover six miles to Umm-es-Samsam. This time, it was the mahelas that delayed us. They could make no headway against the high wind and strong current: although towed by from forty to sixty men each, they did not arrive in camp till after dark. The next day, however, it seemed as though our troubles were over, as the elements were kind to us. On this day, the echelon marched thirteen miles to Shafi, and on the 31st, after a march of twelve and a half miles, reached Filaifilah. On February 1st, we marched nine and a half miles to Ali Gharbi, where a halt was made to draw rations and transfer a few sick men to the field ambulance. The march was continued on the 3rd. Halting for the night near Minthar (16 miles) and Sheikh Saad (12 miles), the echelon arrived at last at Orah (7 miles) on February 5th. Here we found ourselves posted to the old Ferozepore Brigade (now to be called the 7th Brigade), which had been reconstituted,

with the Connaught Rangers, the 27th Punjabis, and the 128th Pioneers as the other units. The Brigade was at that moment holding a portion of the Hannah position, but the Battalion camped for the night in the main camp near Wadi River, and did not move into the trenches until the next night.

Since our arrival in Mesopotamia, numerous cases of sickness were reported. These were put down chiefly to the drinking of Tigris water, but the rain-soaked atta may have had a lot to do with it. No paulins were available to cover the men's rations, with the result that they got into an awful state. To complete the discomfiture of the Medical Officer, an epidemic of mumps broke out in the Battalion. But, in spite of this and of all the hardship that were experienced, only twenty-four men had been transferred to the field ambulance since landing in Basra.

The Battalion spent from February 6th till the 8th in the trenches at Hannah. During this time, it was employed chiefly in improving the existing trenches making dug-outs and constructing communication trenches to the piquets in front of the front line trenches. Three Sepoys were wounded during this period.

On the evening of February 8th, the 7th Brigade was relieved by the 21st Brigade, and we returned to Orah Camp. On the next morning, orders were received to cross to the right bank of the river that same afternoon. At the moment of starting, these orders were cancelled and thereafter orders were received almost daily, and daily cancelled again, so that it was not until the 14th that the Battalion actually moved. The camp on the right bank was known as Camp C, and here we found ourselves welcomed back to the old 3rd (Lahore) Division.

It might be as well here to give an idea of the state in which the force under General Aylmer existed at this time. Anyone who has read the last few pages describing the march of the Battalion up the Tigris can estimate the reliability of the road communications. The only other form of transport communication (other than by air) was by river craft. At that time, there were very few river steamers on the Tigris. With these, supplemented by mahelas, it was all that the Supply and Transport Corps and Ordnance Department could do to supply us with the bare necessities of life. Units had to send out parties daily to cut brushwood in lieu of firewood, and other rations were cut down to the bare minimum, although a generous scale of rations was authorised by Corps orders. This state of affairs existed until well on in July, when communications were improved by stretches of light railway and the arrival of several more river steamers.

On the night of the 15th/16th, the Battalion took part in a "side show". The village of Said Hashim was suspected of harbouring enemy spies. The village was surrounded during the night, and, at dawn, was searched carefully. No strangers were found in the village, however, so we marched back to breakfast and a sleep.

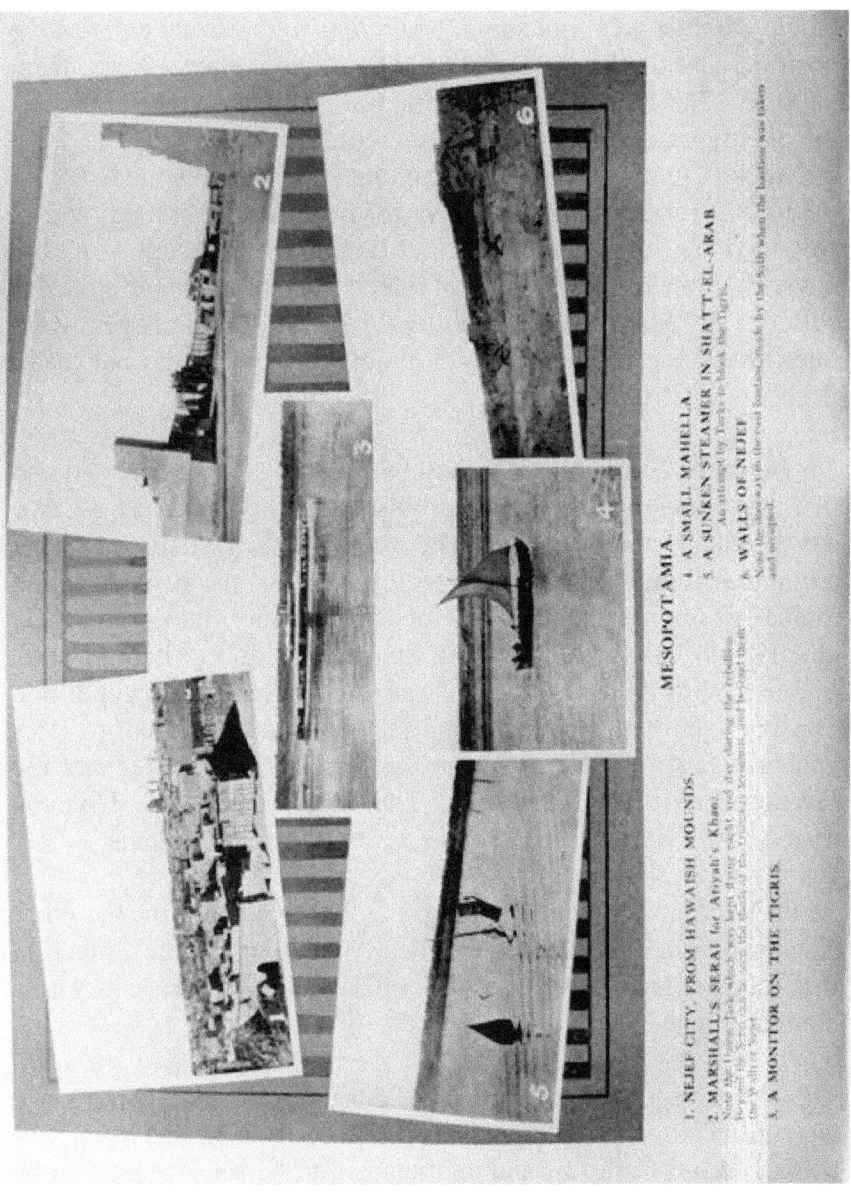

MESOPOTAMIA

1. NEJEF CITY, FROM HAWAISH MOUNDS.
2. MARSHALL'S SERAI (at Ariyah's Khan).
   Near the Hinna Jetty, where men kept day and day during the rebellion,
   beyond the Serai and is one of the islands of the Ayemean Steamer, and beyond them
   the walls of Nejef.
3. A MONITOR ON THE TIGRIS.
4. A SMALL MAHELA
5. A SUNKEN STEAMER IN SHATT-EL-ARAB
   An attempt by Turks to block the Tigris.
6. WALLS OF NEJEF
   Note the inroads in the west fashion, made by the Sufis when the fashion was taken
   and occupied.

Our transport and officers' chargers not having arrived from France, 56 mules and 9 carts, with Indian drivers complete, were attached to the Battalion on February 17th. The same day, the whole Brigade went out some three miles to construct a defensive position near the Sanna Canal (19 D.). We were out all day, from 0800 to 1730 hours. But the work was somewhat interrupted by the enemy cavalry, assisted by some infantry, estimated at from 200 to 400. Our own casualties amounted to 2 men wounded, whilst the enemy were known to have lost 3 killed and 2 wounded. In this operation, the Battalion was supplying the covering force to the Brigade, of which none of the other units suffered any casualties. On February 19th, the Brigade again went out to work on the Sanaa. position, but this time we did not suffer from any interruptions.

On February 20th, orders for certain operations were received and then, later, postponed. But, after this, we always had to have two days' cooked rations in hand. The next day, the Battalion, leaving a dump at Camp C moved out with the rest of the Brigade to the Sanna position, which they; occupied. The dump consisted chiefly. of clerks, followers and men left behind to help to cook rations. With this depot also was the Battalion's second line transport. Out at Sanna, more labour was expended on this position. Later In afternoon the 8th h and 9th Brigades and the Divisional Artillery joined us. That night the whole Division marched to the bend of the river near Abu Roman Mounds.

At 0630 hours the next morning, the Turkish camp on the other side of the river was treated to an early morning "strafe", much to their consternation. A good deal of damage was caused by this bombardment.

The Division remained here , and, during the next few days, we were all busy constructing a new position. Rations had to be sent up daily from Camp C, and animals had to be sent back as far as Mud Fort to water and only atnight could this be done with any degree of safety. The 23rd passed quietly, the 7th Brigade being in Divisional reserve. On the 24th, orders received to extend the left of the 9th Brigade were suddenly postponed, and, instead, the

Connaught Rangers and ourselves were ordered to clear Baddu's Bend of snipers, who were annoying our artillery. The whole area was quickly searched, but without any success. The Machine Gun Section, A Company, and half of B Company (six platoons) were left in position near the river bank to keep down the fire of the enemy, from the other bank. The remainder of us returned to take up a position on the left of the 9th Brigade. Casualties in this show were 2 other ranks killed and 18 wounded.

The result of all these operations was that the Division was occupying an entrenched position, with its right on the bank of the Tigris near Abu Roman Mounds and its left flank stretching out
towards the Umm-el-Brahm. This position was known as the Abu Roman position.

Here we remained until March 7th. We were by no means confined to our trenches, and so a good deal of attention was paid to close-order drill and instruction in grenades and machine gun classes.

On March 5th, Lieutenant-Colonel Campbell rejoined and took over command of the Battalion, but the next day left to take command of the 9th Brigade again.

On March 7th, orders were received for the long-expected operations. A force composed of five brigades, with the 3rd and 7th Divisional Artillery, assembled near the Abu Roman position on the evening of the 7th. During the night, the column made a brilliant night march and advance into positions allotted for each unit preparatory to a combined attack on the flank of the Es Sinn position. The objective finally allotted to the 7th Brigade was the Sinn Abtar Redoubt. Our attack was to start when the assault on the Dujailah Redoubt by the 8th Brigade had been driven home. At 0530 hours, the Brigade reached a point about 40 b 2.7. Here we wheeled to the right, and advanced in a westerly direction. The Brigade was now formed with the 27th Punjabis and 128th Pioneers leading, with the Connaught Rangers in echelon to the right, and the 89th on the left, Artillery formation was adopted by the Battalion, and the whole Brigade moved forward until we reached a point about 2,000 yards from Dujailah Redoubt. \here we halted on the left of one of our own batteries. The Turks did not seem to realise that anything unusual was occurring until about 0700 hours, when the artillery began their preliminary bombardment of the Turkish position and the camps beyond. The general opinion was that, if our force had advanced steadily on, it would have met with but little resistance. However, the artillery carried out their bombardment according to a prearranged schedule, which occupied most of the day.

At 1015 hours, scouts were sent out from the Battalion to reconnoitre the ground over which we were to attack. It was while on this duty that No.2278 Lance-Naik Santa Singh, with a patrol of three men, showed great initiative in am bushing a patrol of six enemy and bringing back five of them prisoners. 'this feat was accomplished within 250 yards of the enemy trenches I

At 1715 hours, the 8th Brigade launched their attack on Du Jailah. This attack was carried out amidst a storm of hostile fire, so that very few reached the Turkish trenches; fewer still returned. Our attack therefore was not carried out. ·

At 1930 hours, the Battalion had to furnish outposts for the night on a frontage of about 2,000 yards, and, as no touch could be gained with the 8th Brigade on our left and no troops were on our right, both our flanks were in the air. We were also all feeling the lack of drinking water; so the water mules with their pakhals were sent off under a British officer to find some. This party succeeded only in losing itself in the dark, and did not rejoin until the next day.

Next day, the force withdrew to Camp C. The 89th, being the last to leave, covered the initial withdrawal. Our retirement began about 1230 hours, passing through the 27th Punjabis about 1,000 yards in our rear. Finally, the whole Brigade fell back, passing through the 35th and 37th Brigades, holding a position two miles back. The retirement was carried out in a most orderly manner. At 1800 hours, the Brigade reached the Pools of Siloam (a group of twelve wells). Here the animals were watered, and the men had their first drink since the night before. Although the day had been warm, only one man had fallen out on the way. Our casualties only amounted to two men wounded.

An incident worthy of mention may be told here of how No.1766 Havildar Jagdeo Dube (previously mentioned in France) displayed great endurance during this day's work. During the artillery duel on the previous day, he received a shrapnel bullet in his right' knee but, like Subedar Ma or Sundar Singh, he carried on with his duty. Going on picquet duty with his section that night, he marched and commanded them in action all the next day, and only went to the aid post when ordered to do so by .his Company Commander on the night of March 9th/10th.

The Abu Roman position was now left unoccupied, and the force retired to Camp C, leaving the 7th Brigade occupying Sanna.

On the 10th it was discovered that the Turks had occupied Abu Roman, so it was decided to try to dislodge them. At 0300 hours on the 11th orders were received for the 7th Brigade to occupy Thorny Nullah. In conjunction with the Connaught Rangers, the 89th moved off at 0350 hours. The Rangers had orders to occupy Thorny Nullah 400 yards north and south of the point where the track crosses it, and we were to continue the line up the *nullah* to the junction of it with the Tigris, and also occupy Maxim Mounds. There was one battalion still occupying Twin Canals as an advanced post. This battalion was to cooperate with our advance by occupying the *nullah* on the left of the Rangers.

Orders issued to companies by Colonel Geoghegan were briefly as follows : On arrival at position of deployment, D Company (double company), leading, to move forward and extend Rangers' line to the right. The other three companies to follow at 150 yards distance in rear of right of D Company, in the following order, B, C, A. On arrival at Thorny Nullah, D Company to inform B, who would move up on right of D, and extend to right as far as the Tigris. At the same time C would wheel northwards and occupy Maxim Mounds. A Company to halt and remain in reserve.

At 0530 hours the Rangers and the 89th deployed and at 0615 hours the Turks got alarmed and opened fire. It appears that in the dark, the leading companies had crossed Thorny Nullah without being aware of it. This was very easy to do, as the *nullah* was a broad dry depression which might easily not be noticed in the dark.

When the Turks opened fire, D and B Companies formed up on the right of the Rangers and both battalions, ignoring the heavy rifle fire directed on them, advanced gallantly to the assault.

Driving in the enemy's advanced troops, they charged and occupied the enemy's front line trench. In the meanwhile C Company, who were following B, and were without information as to what was happening, left one platoon facing north to protect the flank and advanced in support. The fourth company, A, took up a position in Thorny Nullah, where Battalion Headquarters was established. By 0630 hours touch with the Rangers was lost, but B and D Companies had well established themselves in the Turkish trenches and a firefight was commenced. Captain Wood was severely wounded while gallantly leading bombing party up a communication trench towards the enemy second line trench. He was subsequently taken prisoner, together with his orderly Bhagwan Singh, who showed great devotion by refusing to leave him. Twice the enemy retired, but on reinforcements coming up, was able to return and maintain his position. Both our flanks were now exposed, and the position of these two gallant companies was becoming very precarious. At 0745 hours, the only British officer remaining (who was also wounded) gave orders to withdraw to Thorny Nullah. All wounded who could possibly be sent back were evacuated, and the remnants fell back in magnificent order, under the command of Subedar Zaman Shah and Colour-Havildar (now Subedar) Ghulam Muhammed.

Meanwhile, Second Lieutenant Wadley who had been sent to find touch with the Connaught Rangers, had done off to the left, where he and his orderly dropped into a trench full of Turks. Fortunately these were just on the point of surrendering to the Connaught Rangers, who had surrounded them. On Second Lieutenant Wadley's appearance, they threw down their rifles and were finally handed over to the Rangers whose prisoners they really were.

Many deeds of heroism were performed in this action, and it is hard to choose which to chronicle. The determination of Subedar Zaman Shah left in command of B Company, and Colour-Havildar Ghulam Muhammed, in command of D Company, in maintaining their precarious position in face of all odds, their steadiness and coolness, which inspired such confidence in their men, and their marked ability in handling the withdrawal when ordered to retire, is beyond all praise. On our left, when touch was lost with the Connaught Rangers, No.2370 Lance-Naik Amir Dad twice made his way over open ground, under intense rifle fire, to that battalion, thus maintaining communication with them. On the left flank also, No.2578 Sepoy Sher Muhammed had made his way up a communication trench, and from this advanced position kept throwing grenades until the supply was finished; by so doing he checked an attempt by the enemy to turn our left flank. After his bombs were finished he rendered valuable service by collecting ammunition from casualties and distributing it along the firing line. Then in the centre we have No.1841 Lance-Naik Mahtab Ali, who five times jumped out of the trench he was in, and, each time under intense fire from the enemy, brought in a wounded man from a small fold in the ground in front. He was himself severely wounded when bringing in the fifth man. On the right of the line, No.1653 Havildar Gurdit Singh, who had assumed command of his platoon after his commander had been wounded, showed ability during the withdrawal. His platoon being the last to withdraw, he remained in position and drove back repeated efforts of the enemy to follow up the withdrawal, and eventually brought his platoon back in excellent order. After the withdrawal, No.1218 Bugle-Major Bahadur went forward twice, under heavy rifle fire, and each time brought in a wounded man.

By 0920 hours our line was established on the edge of Thorny Nullah. C Company on the right, A on the left, with the remnants of B and D in reserve. The Connaught Rangers on our left and, in the evening, the 128th Pioneers on our right rear, secured our flanks.

The Battalion casualties during the operation at Es Sinn on the 8th and 9th were 1 British officer (Captain Burnett) slightly wounded and 11 Other ranks wounded; while our casualties on the morning of the 11th were:-

Killed-Subedar Chainchal Singh and 14 other ranks.

Missing all believed killed – 9 other ranks.

Missing and wounded – Capt Wood, Jemadar Khan Muhammed and 23 other ranks.

Missing – 41 other ranks.

and

Wounded – Major Geoghegan, Captain Burnett, Second Lieutenants Humphrey and Peto, Subedar Saide Khan and Jemadars Bagga Singh, Kishun Singh and Madat Khan and 124 other ranks.

We afterwards heard that Captain Wood died of wounds in hospital in Baghdad. A good and fearless soldier, his death was a great loss to the 89th, and was universally regretted. Our total casualties in this show were 5 British officers, 6 Indian officers and 211 other ranks nearly all from B and D Companies. It is interesting to compare the above with the official account which was published in the papers soon after :-

> The following report has been received from General Lake on the operations in Mesopotamia : On the 10th March information was received by the Tigris Corps that the Turks had occupied an advanced, position on the Tigris, and a column was sent before dawn on the 11th March to turn the enemy out. The infantry assaulted the position and bayoneted considerable numbers of Turks, and the column then withdrew with two Turkish officers and fifty men as prisoners. There are no further developments to report.

The next day (12th) our position was organised in depth, with the Rangers still on our left, the 27th Punjabis on our right, and the 128th Pioneers in reserve. A line of picquets was pushed out 200 yards in front of Thorrny Nullah. The 13th passed quietly, no action being taken by either side. That night, the firing line advanced up to the picquet line and dug in, while the picquets moved forward another 200 yards, and the support line came up and occupied Thorny Nullah. The remnants of D Company were absorbed in those of B, and the whole organised as one company.

On the night of the 15th/16th, the 27th Punjabis took and held Mason's Mounds without much difficulty. The Brigade now held the line, Mason's Mounds-Twin Canals. The next week passed uneventfully, the position was improved daily, only a few casualties occurring. From the 12th until the 23rd, two other ranks died of wounds, and Subedar Bakshish Singh and 33 other ranks were wounded. Three officers orderlies were reported missing. These men were carrying food up to the firing line to their respective sahibs; the front line was not continuous and they scorning to follow the communication trench, must have missed their way in the dark and walked into the enemy trench. The enemy opened rapid fire at them believing we were making a raid. It was afterwards learnt that two were killed and one was taken prisoner. In him the battalion lost a very good hockey goalkeeper.

All who have been in Mesopotamia will remember how the melting of the snows on the mountains affects the flooding of the Tigris. These floods were now to cause both the Turks and ourselves a great deal of discomfort. On March 24th the river began to overflow its banks and the flood appeared in No Man's Land. All men in the firing line and supports were busily employed in heightening and strengthening their parapets to keep out the flood. By the evening of the 24th, the greater part of our trenches had to be evacuated; their loss was immaterial to us as the Turks on their side were equally inconvenienced. We were relieved by the 47th Sikhs on the night of the 25th. The period ,up to April 5th was uneventful. Second Lieutenant O'Reilly and Subedar-Major Sundar Singh, with some of the transport personnel, whom we had last seen at Lillers in December, rejoined on March 26th, but all animals and carts had been left behind at Basra.

On April 5th, at 0400 hours, the Brigade paraded and moved up to, carry out an advance, the launching of which was dependent on the success of the 13th Division (General Maude's) in their attack on the Hannah position. The Brigade moved up as far as

Thorny Nullah. Here we remained until, at 1200 hours, in conjunction with the 37th Brigade, we advanced and carried an enemy trench. At 1500 hours, we consolidated on a line running approximately north-west to south-east through a point about 18 d 2.5.

The enemy to our front and left flank now kept us anxiously busy, and many alarming reports, were received, but none of the threatened counter-attacks were carried out, and nothing worse than long-range shrapnel fire was experienced by the Battalion. At
1830 hours, being relieved by the 27th Punjabis, the 89th were sent to take over a position on the left of the line from the 9th Gurkhas. This relief was completed in the dark. The Battalion found themselves holding a picquet line about a mile in extent.
The next morning the picquets were withdrawn as soon as our cavalry had passed through. At 1430 hours we had to reoccupy the line. Extra picquets were put out, extending the line another few hundred yards but the Umm-el-Brahm was still reported to be 1,500 yards to our left. Our flank being thus in the air, the gap was well patrolled during the night. However, after one enemy patrol had been driven off in the early part of the night, there were no further signs of activity in that region.

On the 7th, while an attack was being made on the Sanna-i-Yat position on the left bank of the Tigris, we were ordered to make a reconnaissance in force to locate and estimate the strength of the enemy in old British trenches in 29.C. A Company carried out the reconnaissance, with C Company and one Sub-section of machine guns n support. They discovered that the trench in question was only occupied by enemy cavalry patrols. The reconnaissance caused the enemy some uneasiness. By 1500 hours the enemy cavalry was threatening both flanks of A company. At 1600 hours our own cavalry moved up to protect our left flank but, a quarter of an hour later, withdrew without any warning. Half a hour later the reconnaissance withdrew to their original picquet line just in time to avoid becoming engaged with considerably superior forces. After dark the same evening we had again to alter our line of picquets.

The flood, which up to now had been fairly well kept within bounds began to rise again, and, by the evening of the 8th, all our picquets were surrounded, and the water was only kept out of the trenches by small hastily erected bunds.

On the morning of April 9th, the 7th Brigade concentrated at point 18 d 5.5. We were relieved by a battalion of the 9th Brigade, and then had to march two miles, wading through water one foot deep to the position of concentration, where we bivouacked for the night, forming a perimeter camp on some rising ground.

April 10th passed off quietly, and on the 11th the 89th took over an outpost line from the 27th Punjabis. Nine picquets were occupied by two platoons of B Company on the right, with C Company and No.1 Sub-section machine guns on the left. In reserve were A Company and the two other platoons of B Company, who remained in the perimeter camp. A *nullah* 1200 yards in front of our picquet line was occupied by our patrols that night, as Turkish snipers had made use of it the previous night. B Company patrols came under fire, so the two platoons moved up to occupy the *nullah* in strength. Eventually the whole of B occupied the new position, with C in support 150 yards behind. A Company and Battalion Headquarters moved up to the old picquet line. The new position was afterwards known as Rohde s Picquet, being named after B Company's commander, who sad to relate, was to lose his life the next day.

That night (April 11th/12th) a torrential downpour of rain caused much discomfort, impeded movement, and greatly increased the floods. which were already causing a great deal of a anxiety. During the ensuing period of fighting, owing chiefly to the weather conditions, orders and counter-orders followed each other in quick succession and so, to avoid bewildering the reader, only the bare facts of what was done are related. It is interesting to note that the strength of the battalion on the morning of the 12th was 10 British officers, 12 Indian officers, and 407 other ranks. The reason why such a large proportion of British officers had survived may be put down to the fact that they had always worn pugrees when in action.

Subedar Shahmed Khan V.C

At 1500 hours on April 12th, the 8th and 37th Brigades on our right advanced against the Turkish line. B Company, with C in support, conforming with the movement, advanced in line with the 37th Brigade. The Turks retired some 800 yards, but not without inflicting heavy casualties on B and C Companies. During the advance one platoon of B Company, under Subedar Zaman Shah, was detached some 400 yards to the left, to protect that flank, which was in the air. During this advance, Lieutenant Rohde was killed and Captain Chapman and Second Lieutenant Bates (Machine Gun Officer, who afterwards died of wounds) wounded. This left a newly joined subaltern, Second Lieutenant Denny, commanding the firing line. So at 1830 hours, Captain James moved up with two platoons of A Company to reinforce the firing line. The situation was now roughly as follows: The remnants of B and C Companies (less Subedar Zaman Shah's platoon), with A Company (less two platoons) and three machine guns, were holding a position about 1,000 yards in front of Rohde's Picquet. On the right were the 36th Sikhs (37th Brigade). On the left, separated from the rest of the firing line by a gap of about 400 yards, was Subedar Zaman Shah and his gallant platoon, who maintained their position against heavy odds. Covering this gap, and slightly in advance of our line, was Lance-Naik Shahmed Khan with one machine gun. On the left of Subedar Zaman Shah, again, the 27th Punjabis were moving up in support. This fine battalion groped their way forward in the darkness, under very heavy fire, and managed later to gain touch with our left. But for their support and that of that hard fighting regiment the Connaught Rangers, it is very doubtful if we should have been able to maintain our position as we did. At Rohde's Picquet were two platoons of A Company, with Battalion Headquarters in support, and 1,200 yards in rear the Connaught Rangers had moved up and occupied our old picquet line. At 2100 hours, the 8th and 37th Brigades on our right having withdrawn some 800 yards, our right flank was thus exposed. At 2200 hour s, two platoons of the 27th Punjabis relieved Subedar Zaman Shah's platoon. One occupied his picquet, the other attempted to fill up the gap on the right. Subedar Zaman Shah closed on the left of " B "Company. At 2330 hours, two platoons of the Connaught Rangers arrived at Rohde's Piquet, and were sent forward to fill up the gap between us and the 37th Brigade.

At midnight, Lance-Naik Shahmed Khan's gun was knocked out of. action and he was ordered to withdraw , as the gap which he, together with No.237 Sepoy Hukm Dad and No.2306 Fateh Ali, had held against several enemy counter-attacks since 1900 hours, was now filled. For his gallant conduct during this action, Shahmed Khan was promoted Naik on the spot, and was afterwards awarded the Victoria Cross. The other two men, in spite of all recommendations, received nothing. In this action No.2370 Naik Amir Dad again distinguished himself, many times carrying messages from the left flank to the British officer in command of the firing line and going back with instructions which he gave to his platoon commander, the whole time being exposed to very heavy fire. No.1749 Havildar Rampersan Tiwari, who found himself in charge of the Machine Gun Section when Second Lieutenant Bates was mortally wounded, showed marked ability in the tactical dispositions he made for his guns. His gallantry in going from gun to gun, encouraging his men and giving instructions to make the most effective use of their fire, gained for him a well-earned I.O.M. Jemadar Bur Singh (now Subedar-Major), although wounded early in the engagement, showed great gallantry and devotion by crawling up and down the line for four hours, controlling his men and carrying orders from the senior British officer, who was also wounded, but unable to move. Although he could have left the firing line at any time, he only agreed to do so after the last wounded British officer had been removed. No.2254 Havildar Chiragh Din also showed great gallantry in keeping in touch with the platoon on the left. All night long, ammunition carriers were busy carrying ammunition up to the firing line. The most prominent of these were No.2720 Sepoy Saudagar Khan and a Sepoy Nawab Khan, who each brought up 750 rounds of ammunition and showed the greatest contempt for danger by refusing to get into the trench, but walked up and down the firing line coolly distributing their ammunition. The casualties were so heavy that the stretcher-bearers were also working most of the night. When he heard of the state of things in the firing line, our Medical Officer, Lieutenant Sondhi, I.M.S., taking with him No.1647 Lance-Naik Ramdahin Tiwari (the hospital orderly-havildar), went up to the front, and there, out in the open, he gave first aid to all those that were brought_ to him, thus alleviating much suffering and perhaps saving many lives and certainly many limbs, for some of these men could not be evacuated until hours afterwards. Lieutenant Sondhi was granted a M.C. for this action.

Our total casualties on the 12th were:-
Killed – 2 British officers and 15 other ranks.
Wounded – 1 British officer, 3 Indian officers, and 99 other ranks.
Missing – 1 other rank.

At 0230 hours on the 13th, another platoon of A Company was sent up, under Second Lieutenant O'Reilly, to reinforce the firing line. Only one platoon of A Company being now in Battalion reserve, the Rangers were again called upon to help us. By 0330 hours, two more platoons of this regiment arrived; one was pushed forward into the firing line, and the other kept in reserve at Rodhe's Picquet.

By noon on the same day, we discovered that the 37th Brigade, on right, having lost their bearings in the night, had so sighted their trenches as to enfilade our right picquets and those of the Rangers from the rear. This was not corrected until 1700 hours.

Our casualties on the 13th were 3 other ranks killed and 11 wounded.

On April 15th another advance was made. Our Brigade, assisted by the 9th Brigade, assaulted the enemy advanced position to the north of the 89th and were successful in straightening out our line between us and the Tigris. In this attack the only forward movement of the 89th was by patrols. One of these patrols on the left captured an enemy picquet, in which they found six dead Turks, and one survivor whom they made prisoner. At 2000 hours, the Battalion was relieved by the 93rd Burma Infantry, and concentrated at Rohde's Picquet. During the 15th, 8 other ranks were wounded.

April 16th passed quietly, officers and men all enjoying a well-earned rest. At 0145 hours on the 17th, the Battalion marched off to concentrate with the rest of the Brigade, which, with the 9th

Brigade, was to carry out an attack on Beit Aiessa. The two brigades were each allotted a frontage of 300 yards, 7th Brigade on the right, 9th Brigade on the left. The 7th Brigade were drawn up as in the following diagram :-

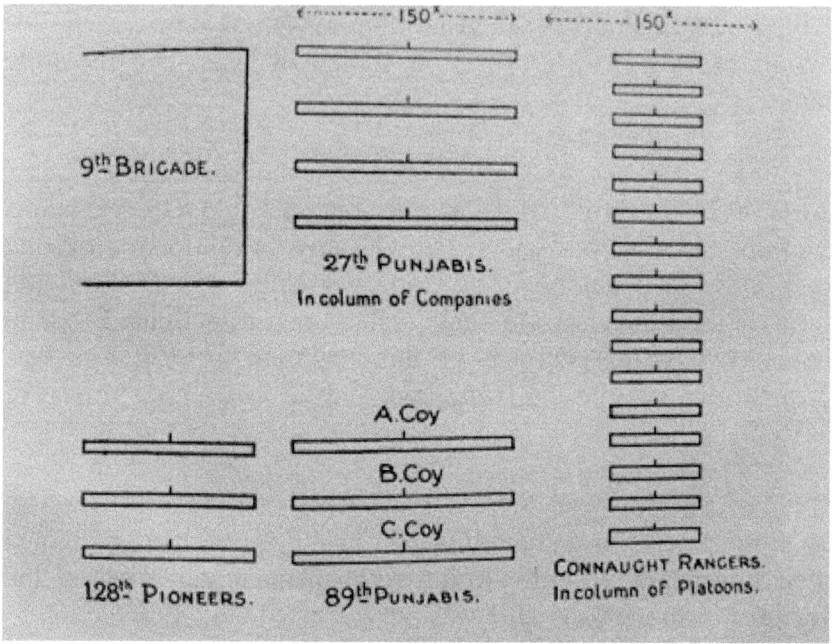

The first line occupied the advanced British trench, and the remaining lines dug themselves in on arrival in position for assault. This position was reached at 0300 hours. At 0700 hours, after a preliminary bombardment by our artillery the Brigade advanced to the assault. The enemy's first and second line trenches were carried by the 27th Punjabis and the leading platoons of the Rangers, and occupied by them. The 89th leap-frogged over, and then making a half right form, carried their own objective, namely, the six mouths of the water channel at Beit Aiessa. This assault was carried out with such dash that the 89th passed clean through our own artillery barrage. During this advance the Battalion lost a brilliant Indian officer in Subedar Zaman Shah, who was killed by a shrapnel bullet in the head, fired by an enemy gun just the other side of the Tigris. Captain James, who was leading with A Company, advanced as far as a small sand hill on the riverbank just west of the sixth channel.

The 89th now started digging in. A Company, with two machine guns, occupied the advanced position, with B Company, under Lieutenant Campbell, in support in the sixth channel; Second Lieutenant O'Reilly, with C Company and the third machine gun (Shahmed Khan's gun had not been replaced) in the fifth channel; Regimental Headquarters in the fourth channel. On our right was the Tigris, and on our left, which was thrown back to join up with the 9th Brigade, were the Connaught Rangers. The day passed uneventfully, and the position gained was consolidated. Any sniping by the enemy was easily dealt with by the machine gun with C Company, leaving the remainder free to dig themselves in. However, strong bodies of Turks could be seen massing near Chahela Trenches, and at 1900 hours a determined Turkish counter-attack developed, and, in spite of tremendous casualties, broke through our line between the 7th and 9th Brigades. But owing to the gallant efforts of the Connaught Rangers and the 128th Pioneers the line was soon mended again, and the enemy withdrew slightly. The position of the Connaught Rangers and the 89th was· now very precarious, so at 0130 hours on the 18th we were ordered to withdraw to the Turkish first line trench captured that morning. This withdrawal was effected, and by 0300 hours the Battalion found themselves crammed in 150 yards of 3 ft. by 3 ft. trench, with the Rangers on the right and a unit of the 39th Brigade on the left. The men were dog-tired; none of them having slept for nearly forty-eight hours, so nothing could be done to improve our position until next day. Behind this trench, the country was all flooded, but on our left, the ground over which we had begun our assault on the 17th was subjected to artillery bombardment all the next day. In spite of this, ammunition carriers and fatigue men of the Battalion brought up small arms ammunition and much-needed grenades, and best of all, our day's rations. Conspicuous amongst these men were No.2588 Sepoy Hazura Singh and No.1773 Sepoy Mit Singh, both of whom made several of these journeys. The grenades which they brought were sent along to the unit on our left, where they were urgently required. In the morning, while supervising the sighting of our machine guns, Captain James was wounded in the arm, and a short time later Jemadar Rure Khan was wounded in the neck.

During the day the 89th widened and deepened the trench they were occupying, and the same night were relieved by a unit of the 39th Brigade. The Battalion marched back to a point 400 yards east of Rohde's Picquet, where we bivouacked for the night.

Beit Aiessa Trenches 16th – 17th April 1916

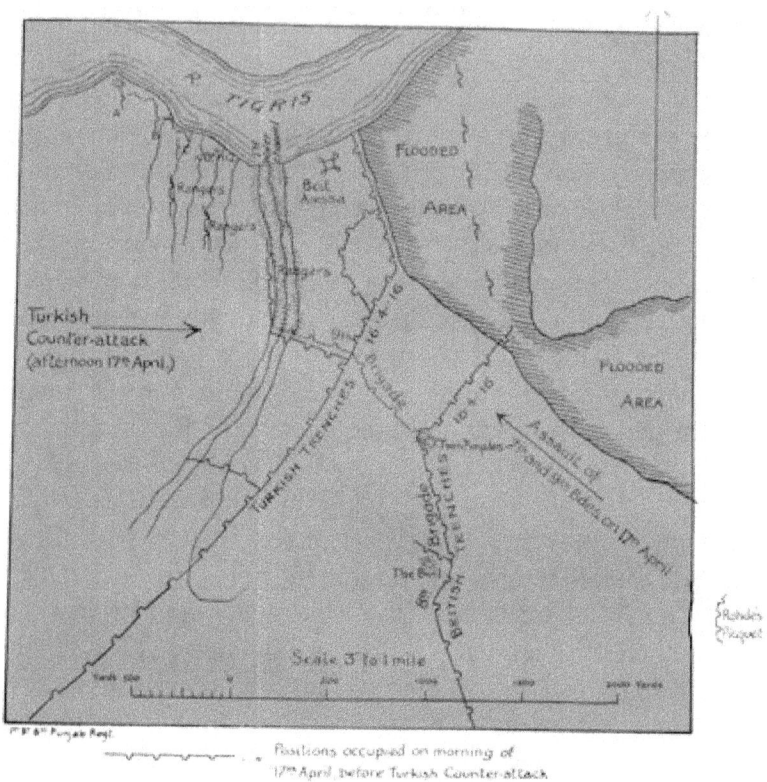

Our casualties on the 17th and 18th were:-
Killed – Subedar Zaman Shah and 4 other ranks.
Wounded – Captain James, Second Lieutenant Denny, Jemadar Rure Khan and 93 other ranks.
Missing – 3 other ranks.
The strength of the Battalion after this period of hard fighting had dwindled to 6 British officers (including the Medical Officer), 6 Indian officers, and 164 other ranks.

In a Special Tigris Corps Order published a few days afterwards, the 89th were "mentioned" among other units for specially distinguished service on the night of April 17th/18th (see Appendix IV).

For five days the Brigade were kept in reserve to the 3rd Division, and, except for having to keep in readiness to move at a moment's notice, were able to rest and reorganise.

The weather was now daily growing hotter, and the flies by day and sand flies by night were becoming a pest. Cholera broke out in the Brigade.

On April 29th the Brigade was relieved, and moved back to a position where tents were allowed us. Here, we were promised a real "rest". On the 30th, the whole Battalion marched to the Tigris, near Mason's Mounds, to bathe and wash their clothes. This was the first real clean up that the men had had since February 19th.

On May 2nd, Brevet-Major R. S. Engledue, whom we had left behind in Gallipoli, rejoined the Battalion, bringing with him a welcome draft of 1 Indian officer and ro4 other ranks. The same day, the whole Brigade was inspected by General Sir Percy Lake, who complimented us all on what we had done.

On May 2nd, Brevet-Major R. S. Engledue, whom we had left behind in Gallipoli, rejoined the Battalion, bringing with him a welcome draft of 1 Indian officer and ro4 other ranks. The same day, the whole Brigade was inspected by General Sir Percy Lake, who complimented us all on what we had done.

Thus ended the last operations to relieve Kut, which fell on April 29th.

On May 8th, a truce was observed between us and the Turks, after the fall of Kut, to allow the steamer Sikkim to proceed to Kut and return loaded with sick and wounded who could not be cared for by the Turks.

On the 9th, Captain J. D. Crawford, who had been Adjutant of the

89th when war broke out, and had carried out his duties as such all through the war with such capability and thoroughness, left the

89th to take up the duties of Staff Captain, 9th Brigade. He left a gap which was hard to fill. Then on the 12th the Brigade lost its General Officer Commanding, General Egerton, who came round to battalions unofficially to say "Good-bye" to British officers and Indian officers, before going to take over command of the 14th Division (see Appendix V). The command of the Brigade fell to Colonel Davidson, D.S.O., 14th Sikhs.

On May 16th, we were inspected by our Divisional General, Major-General Keary, C.B., D.S.O., who presented medals to Captain James and four other ranks.

On May 19th, it was found that the Turks had evacuated all the trenches at Beit Aiessa, and patrols working out towards Sinn Abtar and Dujailah met with no opposition. At 1915 hours, leaving Lieutenant Wadley and 15 other ranks with our tents and heavy kit, the Battalion marched off to the position of assembly of the Brigade, where we halted for the night. At 0500 hours the next morning, the Brigade marched off; passing through the Es Sinn position at 1100 hours, we arrived at Imam-el-Mansur at 1330 hours. The heat was intense, there was a great demand for water, but, by good staff work, this was rushed up shortly afterwards in pakhals loaded on motor lorries, and distributed to units. All our casualties on this march, and the next day's to Magasis, were due to heat-stroke. One man fell dead on the arrival of the Battalion at Imam-el-Mansur, and five others were transferred to field ambulance.

However, by noon on the 21st, tents were pitched and a certain amount of comfort again enjoyed.

On June 4th, Second Lieutenant E. M. Milne, with a draft of 66 other ranks, joined the Battalion. On the 10th, it was with universal regret that we heard of the death of Lord Kitchener.

On the 10th, Second Lieutenant Wadley, and, on the 19th, Second

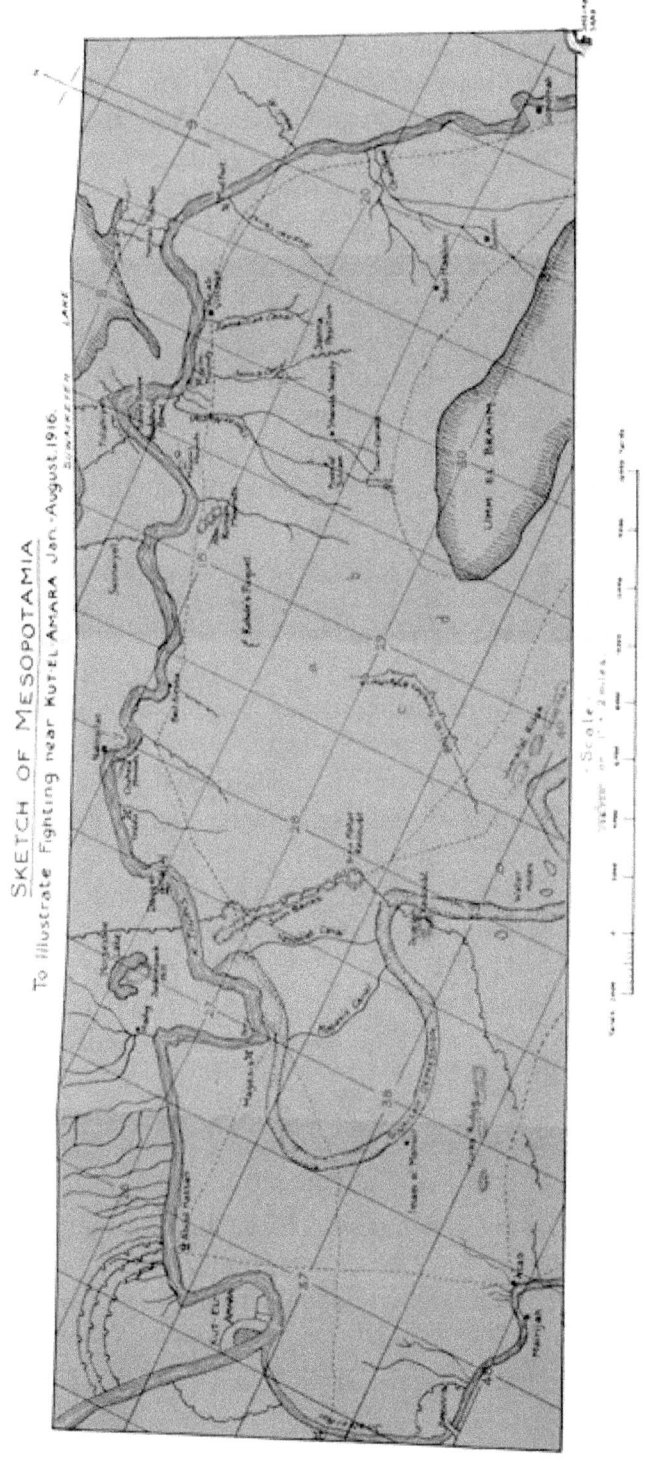

Lieutenant Barnes (who had joined us a few days before), were transferred to field ambulance with fever.

On the 17th, the 89th were relieved by the 37th Dogras. At 0200 hours, we marched back to Twin Canals, where the 7th Brigade were to be concentrated for some time. We reached our new camp at 0815 hours.

Although the Turks had retired on the right bank of the Tigris! they were still holding the Sanna-i-Yat position on the left bank. Thus it was that the Division at Magasis had to be supplied with rations and stores by a daily convoy from Sheikh Saad. This was on the meeting system, with stations at Sodom, Twin Canals, and S.P.4 (one of the strong points on the left flank of the old Beit Aiessa position). Later on, a light railway was completed from Sheikh Saad to Twin Canals, where rail-head was organised.

When the Brigade arrived at Twin Canals, rations were found to be very short. So working parties were organised to cut the crops, which were fairly abundant round about. Drinking water had to be brought from the Tigris. All transport animals were utilised for this purpose, making a trip in the morning and again in the evening. The water was stored in our tarpaulin tanks and treated by the doctor. Animals were watered twice a day when they were at the river.

On June 26th, the Battalion marched out to S.P.4. to take over the line of picquets there. We were spread over a front of about 3,000 yards, our role being chiefly to guard against marauding Arabs. Three days later we were reinforced by one company of the 9th Berar Infantry.

On the morning of the 30th, a number of horses belonging to the 33rd Cavalry, while out grazing near Dujailah, stampeded, and could be seen galloping across our front. Some of them, attracted by our tents, charged our wire entanglement; strange to say, only two or three were badly cut and damaged. Sixty-five were caught by the sepoys, and later handed over to the sowars who came for them.

We were relieved, again by the 93rd Burma Infantry, on July 2nd, and rejoined the Brigade at Twin Canals. The next day we heard that the 89th were to go back for a spell in India to recuperate. Our days were now spent, sometimes at work on the defences of Twin Canals and the railway to Sheikh Saad, and regularly on convoy duty between Sodom and S.P.4.

On July 30th, a Special Brigade Order of the Day was published, and on the next day the Battalion was inspected, by Major-General Keary, C.B., D.S.O., commanding the Lahore Division, who addressed the Battalion and also published a complementary farewell order (see Appendix VI).

On August 1st at 0400 hours, the battalion began its march to Sheikh Saad en route for India. Some difficulty was experienced on arrival at Sheikh Saad, owing to a dust-storm. But rations were finally drawn, and embarkation on River Steamer *P.1* completed by midday.

Margil was reached early on August 4th. The next morning we left in Bamora for Basra, where we picked up our heavy kit in the dump left there. We also took on board 200 Persian coolies to Bunderabbas.

We arrived at Karachi on the 13th, and left for Nowshera the next day.

Our sepoys accustomed to travel in packed railway carriages, were surprised to find that not only was ample space reserved for them in the train, but large blocks of ice, soda water, and hand fans were provided for them. This was the result of what was known as the Karachi troop train tragedy of a week before, when some men of a British draft had died from heat stroke in the Scinde Desert.

Chapter VII
NORTH-WEST FRONTIER OF INDIA 1916–1917

When the Battalion arrived in Nowshera, the Depot, then under the command of Captain W. S. J. Scruby, was still stationed at Dinapore, where it had been ever since the departure of the Battalion on service.

Owing to an outbreak of cholera at Dinapore, it was not until about three weeks later that they were allowed to join the Battalion.

Soon after the arrival of the Depot at Nowshera, all Indian ranks of the Battalion were sent off en bloc for two months' war leave to their homes. The depot was able to provide enough trained sepoys to find guards and duties.

However, in October, before the two months were over, the Battalion was called upon to find two companies to garrison Nagoman and Adozai, two bridgeheads on the road from Peshawar to Shabkadr, with orders to march the same day as escort to a battery of R.F.A., which was on its way to Peshawar. Two companies were quickly organised from trained recruits and sepoys. The column started off the same evening, and, marching most of the night, arrived at Peshawar early the next morning. The accomplishment of this march with no casualties or stragglers was considered a pretty good performance. The majority of the men had not more than twelve months' service, and the march had

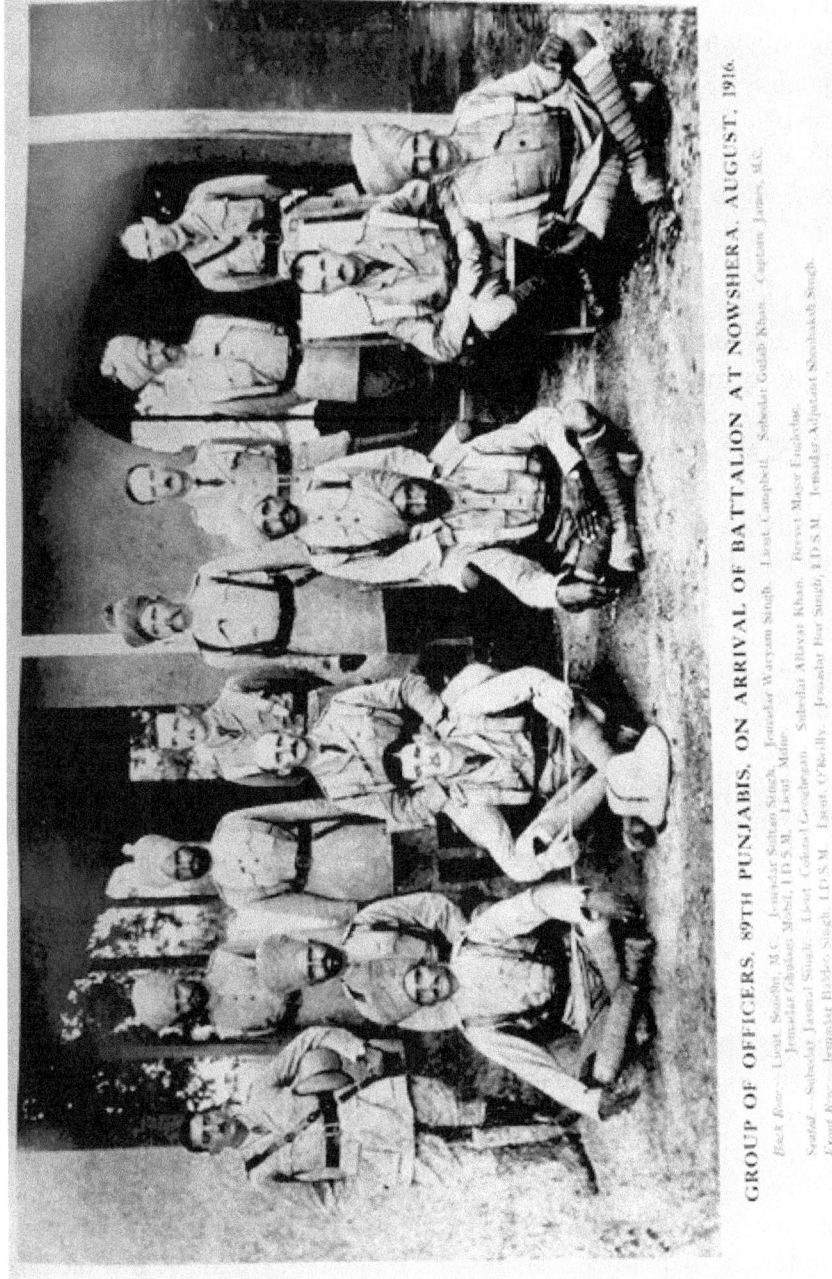

GROUP OF OFFICERS, 89TH PUNJABIS, ON ARRIVAL OF BATTALION AT NOWSHERA, AUGUST, 1916.

Back Row.— Lieut. Sandhu, M.C. Jemadar Sultan Singh. Jemadar Waryam Singh. Lieut Campbell. Subedar Gulab Khan. Captain James, M.C.
Jemadar Ghulam Mohd, I.D.S.M. Lieut Milne
Seated.— Subedar Jaimal Singh. Lieut. Colson-Greatheart. Subedar Altayar Khan. Brevet Major Enderbe.
Front Row.— Jemadar Baldeo Singh, I.D.S.M. Lieut. O'Reilly. Jemadar Bur Singh, I.D.S.M. Jemadar Adjutant Shotokah Singh.

to be made in darkness and in clouds of dust.

In November the men returned from war leave, but we were not to be left to our own devices in Nowshera for long. At the beginning of December, the detachments on the Peshawar-Shabkadr road returned, and the whole Battalion, leaving a Depot to carry on office work and training of recruits in Nowshera, moved to Mardan to relieve a battalion of the Guides, who went into camp near Nowshera for training and manoeuvres.

At Mardan, British officers were all under canvas, but we were able to make ourselves comfortable. Here Christmas was spent. Regimental sports were held in the afternoon, and a ladies' guest night in the mess tent the same evening.

At the conclusion of the manoeuvres, the Battalion, being relieved by the Guides, returned to Nowshera.

Scarcely had we returned, however, before we received orders to proceed at once to Shabkadr Fort, to relieve the 46th Punjabis on the Mohammed Blockade Line.

On February 12th 1917, the battalion marched off from Nowshera. After halting for one night each at Pabbi, Peshawar and Adozai, Shabkadr was reached at 1000 hours on the 15th, and we proceeded at once to take over duties from the 46th Punjabis.

The blockade line was then under the command of Brigadier-General T. G. Woodyat, and was composed of a line of strong points stretching from Abazai Fort, on the Swat River, to Michni Fort, on the banks of Kabul, protected by a continuous belt of barbed wire and at night by an apron of live wire electrically controlled from Shabkadr Fort. This was the first time that wire had been used on the frontier. A few Mohmands were killed by it at first, but they soon learnt to tackle it, either with insulated wire cutters or by putting a rope round it and breaking it. A few jackals and other animals were also electrocuted.

By 1300 hours the relief was complete. We found ourselves, with one company finding garrisons for seven strong points on the blockade line and the other three companies and Battalion Headquarters in reserve at Shabkadr Fort. Guard duties were very heavy and fatigues were numerous, so there was always plenty of work to do. However, duties were so arranged that Company Commanders should get their full company, for training purposes, every third day.

On March 1st, a small punitive expedition was carried out against the villages of Jahangirpura and Wazirkalai. A force, made up of one company and a machine gun section of the 2nd/4th Border Regiment, the 1st Royal Sussex Regiment, the 72nd Punjabis, and H Company, with our machine guns, under Major Scruby, with other details of sappers and miners, signals and ambulance, marched out, under the Brigade Commander at 0500 hours. The two villages were burnt to the ground, towers blown up and walls levelled, and the force returned twelve hours later, having carried out their mission successfully and without any casualties.

At 1500 hours on March 3rd, the 89th, in turn, was relieved by the 55th Cokes Rifles. The next day we began the march back to Nowshera, where we arrived at 1145 hours on the 7th.

Although we had long hoped for a chance to carry out some much-needed training we were not left in peace for long. On March 30th, we received orders' to go back to Shabkadr, and to relieve the 55th Rifles again.

On April 2nd, the Battalion left Nowshera, arriving at Shabkadr on the 5th. The same duties as before were soon taken over form the 55th Rifles, and we settled down to the usual routine.

On April 10th, we were honoured by the presence of the viceroy, Lord Chelmsford, who paid a visit to the blockade line. While His Excellency was inspecting one of our picquets in the line, firing was heard not very far off, to the great alarm of the Staff. This, however, was found to be due to some inter-tribal dispute over some cattle thefts.

On the night of April 21st/22nd, a party of Mohmands, trying to get through the line, were discovered by a patrol and driven off by fire from one of the picquets, but it was feared that no casualties were inflicted. A covering party of the enemy fired on the picquet in reply to our fire, but without any effect.

Two nights later the enemy again tried to get through, and were again driven off. This time at least one of their number was wounded.

Early on the 26th, the Battalion, being relieved by the 38th Dogras, marched off to Peshawar, and eventually arrived at Nowshera at 1000 hours on the 28th.

In June, a draft[1], composed chiefly of non-commissioned officers and a nucleus of old soldiers, was sent to Ferozepore, under Captain Chapman. This draft, together with similar drafts from other of our linked battalions, was organised to form the 2nd Battalion 89th Punjabis, under Lieutenant- Colonel Alexander, and later under Lieutenant-Colonel Oldfield.

At the beginning of September, Colonel Campbell came back to us as Commandant. We were now under orders to accompany the Chitral Relief

Column as escorting unit; to march up as far as Mirkhani with the 11th Rajputs and to return with the 3rd Brahmans.

The column was under orders to march on September 16th, under the command of Brigadier-General D. C. Andrew. But in order to avoid the heat of the day and making the first day's march too long, orders were received at 1520 hours on the 15th to pass the bridge-head of the boat- bridge over the Kabul River at 1830 hours. This point was half an hour's march from the lines. Transport consisted solely of pack mules which had not lately been accustomed to carrying loads. They were consequently very fresh. This freshness wore off in two or three days.

In spite of all unpreparedness, the Battalion marched off from the

---

[1] 1 British officer, 2 Indian officers, 170 other ranks, and 6 followers

lines at 1815 hours, and passed the starting point only a quarter of an hour late. Other units comprising the column arrived at the same time or shortly afterwards, and the whole column marched some six or seven miles along the Mardan Road and then bivouacked for the night on the side of the road.

The next morning, the march was continued at 0500 hours, and we finally reached Mardan at 0715 hours. On September 17th, The column marched to Jalala. As the roads were very dusty, echelon B, second line transport, and the supply column, with a suitable escort, marched one and a half hours ahead of the rest of the column. On the 18th, Dargai was reached, and the next day the column marched to Chakdara Fort.

On this latter march, the transport and its escort proceeded by the graded road, whilst the remainder of the column marched by the old Buddhist road. The Divisional Commander, General Sir F. Campbell, K.C.B., D.S.O. who was on his way to inspect the troops under training near Chakdara, took the salute whilst the column marched past him through Malakand.

A halt was made at Chakdara for two nights.

For the next six days the march was continued. Halts were made at the police posts at Kuzserai, Sadu, Robart, Warai and Dir.

During the march from Sadu to Robart, rain fell heavily all the time, converting dry *nullah* beds quickly into roaring torrents. It was with the greatest difficulty that the rearguard managed to bring in all the transport before dark.

The road after Sadu became very bad, and in some places could hardly be recognised as a road at all.

Arriving at Dir on September 26th, the 89th remained in camp on the 27th, while the remainder of the column continued the march to Chitral. The reason for this was that the camping grounds after Dir were not large enough to hold the whole column. We followed up on the 28th, however, so as to be within helping distance in case of need.

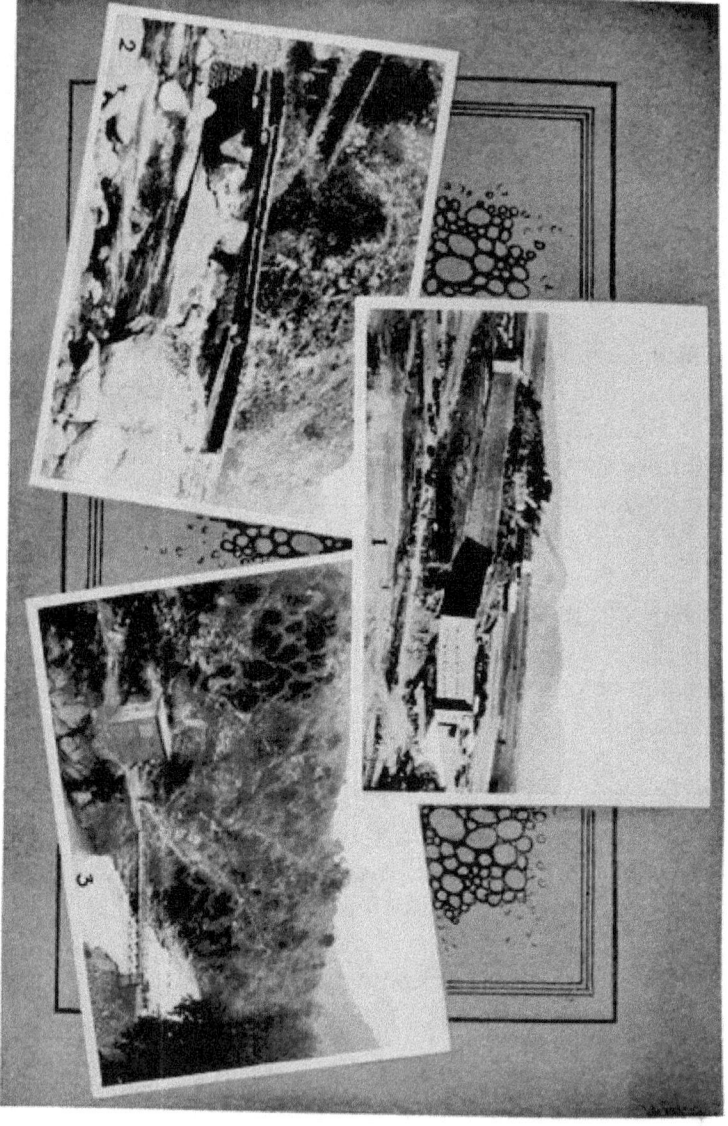

ON THE WAY TO CHITRAL.
1. CHAKDARA FORT
2. CANTILEVER BRIDGE, NEAR DIR
3. BRIDGE AND LEVY POST, NEAR DIR

Halts were made at Mirga on the 28th, and Ziarat on the 29th. Our destination, Mirkhani, was reached finally on September 30th.

The march from Mirga to Ziarat was perhaps the most interesting. During this march one passes from Dir territory into Chitral, over the Lowari Pass (altitude 10,250 feet). The march is one of nine miles, but this includes a climb of 3,000 feet to the summit of the pass and a drop of the same to Ziarat. Great attention was paid to the harness and saddlery of the mules, and, owing to the great care taken, not a single sore back was reported.

The superiority of the roads in Chitral to those we had lately been experiencing was the first thing we noticed after crossing the pass.

The Battalion remained in camp at Mirkhani until the morning of October 6th. During this time ordinary parades were carried out daily. Many men went sick with fever, and the place altogether seemed unhealthy. Several of us took advantage of an afternoon's leave to go for a ride into Kila Drosh to see the place.

On the 6th, we began our return march. That night, at Ziarat, shortly after the British officer of the day had turned out the guard and visited the perimeter sentries, a rifle was stolen from one of the sentries whose post was close to a tree on the perimeter. Leaving him with the broken end of his chain hanging to his belt. Within fifteen seconds the inlying picquet, who were sleeping in the open and close by the sentry, had fallen in and sent two or three rounds rapid down a steep wooded *khud* in the direction the thief had disappeared, but without effect. This incident cast a gloom over the Battalion which was hard to throw off.

On the 8th, the Battalion arrived back at Dir, where a halt was made for two nights to allow the 1st Brahmans to catch us up. Darora was reached by the whole column on the 10th, and on the day following we arrived at Warai. On arriving at this place, a telegram was received by runner from Chakdara, intimating that the 89th were under orders to proceed on field service, once more, in November.

Four more uneventful days of marching brought us back again to

Chakdara, and four days later (October 19th) the 89th led the column into Nowshera.

We had arrived in Nowshera fourteen months previously with the idea of putting the Battalion through some organised training. Owing to our travels during this period, this had hardly been possible except in a disconnected sort of way. However, whatever else had happened, the esprit de corps had in no way deteriorated, and it was with the same high spirits as in October, 1914, that the Battalion entrained for Karachi in two special trains on the evening of November 26th (see Appendix VII).

A Depot was left in Nowshera, under Lieutenant Wadley. They were shortly afterwards transferred to Kamptee, where they remained until the Battalion returned to India in 1920.

The Battalion was now properly organised in companies and platoons, the company letters being A, C, F and H, and Z being the Headquarter Company.

On arrival at Karachi on November 29th, five cases of mumps were reported, which necessitated the isolation of two platoons of H Company. Later, more cases, this time in C Company, were reported, so that finally, when the 89th embarked on H.T. *Ekma* at 0800 hours on December 2nd, 2 Indian officers and 189 other ranks had to be left behind, in the isolation camp.

Before embarking, the Battalion received a telegram of farewell and good wishes from H.E. the Commander-in-Chief in India.

By midday on December 2nd, the embarkation being complete, the ship sailed for Basra.

GROUP OF OFFICERS 1st 89TH PUNJABIS, NOWSHERA, NOVEMBER, 1917.

Back Row— Lieut. Ede, Subedar Sultan Singh, Jemadar Nigam Tar, Lieut. Gordon, Jemadar Beant Singh, I.D.S.M., Subedar Gulab Khan, Lieut. Paston, Jemadar Bur Singh, I.D.S.M., Jemadar Sher Sobah Singh, Jemadar Nur Mad, 2nd Lieut. Baine.

Standing on Ground— Jemadar Rupejeewan Thego, I.O.M., Jemadar Jiwan Singh, Lieut. Budlock, Lieut. Hennah, Jemadar Ghadari Being, I.D.S.M., Captain Campbell, Jemadar Kirpal Singh, Lieut. Webb, Subedar Boban Hari Dube, Lieut. Lockwood, Captain Scotha, M.C., Subedar Dawar Singh, Jemadar Warrium Singh, Subedar Peter Khan.

Seated— Major Baguley, Subedar Jemand Singh, Captain Chapman, Subedar Sarda Khan, Colonel Campbell, C.M.G., Subedar-Major Baldeo Singh Pathaha, Major Spriby, Jemadar Sultan Singh, Lieut-Colonel N. M. Jacquemont.

Front Row— Jemadar Ruben Singh, 2nd Lieut. Phillips, Jemadar Bakhte Singh, I.D.S.M., Jemadar Kanga Singh, I.D.S.M., 2nd Lieut. Morton, and Lieut. Dick.

Chapter VIII
MESOPOTAMIA DECEMBER 1917 TO OCTOBER 1918

After an uneventful voyage, Basra was reached on the morning of December 7th and the 89th transhipped into two lighters, which were later towed up the river to Nahr Umr, where we arrived at 1910 hours. As we had a two mile march to our camping ground, on arrival at which we were to pitch our own camp, it was decided to stay where we were for the night.

Our disembarkation started at 0600 hours the next morning. Two trains had been allotted to us for transport, while the men marched, carrying their own kits. By 1100 hours, camp had been pitched, and all settled in ship-shape.

We remained at Nahr Umr for a week, during which time the Battalion was employed on a strong bund, which was being constructed for the protection of the camp against future floods.

Classes were also started for training extra Lewis gunners. The establishment of Lewis guns per battalion in Mesopotamia had been raised. And although, through the foresight of Colonel Geoghegan, we had many spare trained gunners in each company, these were now all required to complete the new gun sections.

On December 15th, we started our trip up to Baghdad. Leaving

Nahr Umr in three trains, we arrived at Amara the next morning, and proceeded straightway to embark on T.S. '97' and its complement of two barges. As soon as embarkation was complete, we started off up the Tigris to Kut.

On December 18th, a diversion was caused by fire breaking out in a hold of one of the barges, which was full of coal. Fortunately, when the ship's hose was turned on, it was quickly extinguished.

At 0900 hours on the 19th, Kut was reached, and the Battalion (less F Company and all officers' chargers) entrained for Baghdad.

The next day, we arrived at Hinaidie Camp in pouring rain. No intimation as to our arrival having been received, we experienced a good deal of discomfort before we finally got settled into our own camp twenty-four hours later.

Here we remained until Christmas Eve, when we marched through Bagdad to Iron Bridge (on the right bank). Although the ground was already muddy enough from recent rain, to add to our discomfort it rained heavily all the morning. Some idea of the state of the roads may be gathered from the fact that it took the Battalion three hours to march seven miles.

However, by 1400 hours we were all settled more or less comfortably in camp, together with the other units of our new Brigade. This, the 53rd Brigade, had been newly constituted under the command of Brigadier- General G. A. F. Saunders, D.S.O., and, besides the 89th, was composed of the 1st Bn. 9th Middlesex Regiment, and the 1st/3rd and 1st/7th Gurkhas. Attached to the Brigade, also, was No.5 Company, Sappers and Miners.

On December 30th, Major Engledue, with F Company and the officers' chargers, arrived from Kut, and rejoined the Battalion. A day or two later, Major Engledue left us to join the Dunster Force. He was eventually severely wounded at Baku, while gallantly attempting to hold our entrenched positions outside that place. As a consequence of his departure, Captain Campbell took over command of F Company, while Lieutenant G. C. Hele took over the duties of Adjutant. Another of our officers, Crawford, then a Major on the staff, also went with the Dunster Force as Colonel Commanding the Armoured Cars.

From January 11th to 29th, the Battalion was employed on railway construction work on a length of about eleven miles between Cunningham's Post and Marshall's Bridge on the Diyala River. On January 29th, Lieutenant G. B. Rennick, who had been acting as A.D.C. to General Nightingale, rejoined the Battalion.

Early in February, the Brigade received orders to go to the Hillah area of the Euphrates in relief of another brigade. The 89th had to take over garrison duties from the 84th Punjabis at Kufa, with detachments at two posts of Kifl and Abu Sikhair. On February 7th, we marched off, reaching Kifl on the 11th, a distance of eighty-one miles Here a whole day was spent in crossing the river and taking over duties.

Leaving two platoons of H Company at Kifl, the remainder of the Battalion marched to Kufa on the 13th; and, on the 14th, F Company marched on to Abu Sikhair, to take over the post there, while one platoon of C Company proceeded to the Assistant Political Officer's (Captain Marshall) residence, just outside the city of Nejef, to take over guard duties there. This residence had belonged to a notorious outlaw, named Atiyah, but had been commandeered for the use of the A.P.O., and was known as Atiyah's Khan. After the trouble with Nejef broke out, the name was changed to Marshall's Serai.

Nejef, the sacred shrine of the Shiyah Mohammedans, is about three miles distant from Kufa, and was connected to it by a narrow-gauge horse-tram service.

In addition to ordinary parades and classes, the first few days of our stay at Kufa were occupied in making roads and culverts, throwing up bunds along the river, and improving the existing sanitation.

On March 10th, Colonel L. W. Y. Campbell, C.M.G., gave up

command of the Battalion to take up duties as a Brigade Commander in India. All ranks were very sorry to say good-bye to him. Lieutenant Colonel N. M. Geoghegan again assumed command. It might be mentioned here that, except for the six and a half months for which Colonel Campbell returned as Commandant, Colonel Geoghegan commanded the 89th from November, 1915, until August, 1924, a period of nearly nine years.

For a month, the daily routine of road construction, fatigues and company parades was continued. During this period, Lieutenant F. H. Ledgerwood, who had gone to Kamptee from Nowshera with the Depot, joined the Battalion as reinforcement.

On the evening of March 18th, a telegraph linesman, who was returning to Kufa from a visit to Abu Sikhair, found the telegraph line cut in three places. This, at the time, was thought to be the childish prank of some wandering Arab. But, the next morning, just as we were all preparing for early morning parade, a telephone message from our platoon at Atiyah's

Khan startled us all with the news of the murder of the A.P.O., Captain Marshall, and the wounding of Captain Hampson, an officer of the Labour Corps, who was staying at Atiyah's Khan with Captain Marshall. It was found out later that this was the beginning of a revolt engineered by the Turks themselves, but it was brought to a premature head by some disgruntled *Shabanas* (Arab police), thus marring the success of the Turkish plans.

At 0600 hours on March 19th, the gates of Atiyah's Khan were opened. Outside were the usual number of *Shabanas* waiting to begin their duties for the day. The sepoy sentry moved to his position outside the gate; whereupon he was attacked from behind by three *Shabanas*, who stabbed him and took his rifle; this was recovered later.

Captain Marshall came out of his room near the gate to see what all the noise was about, and was shot dead. Captain Hampson

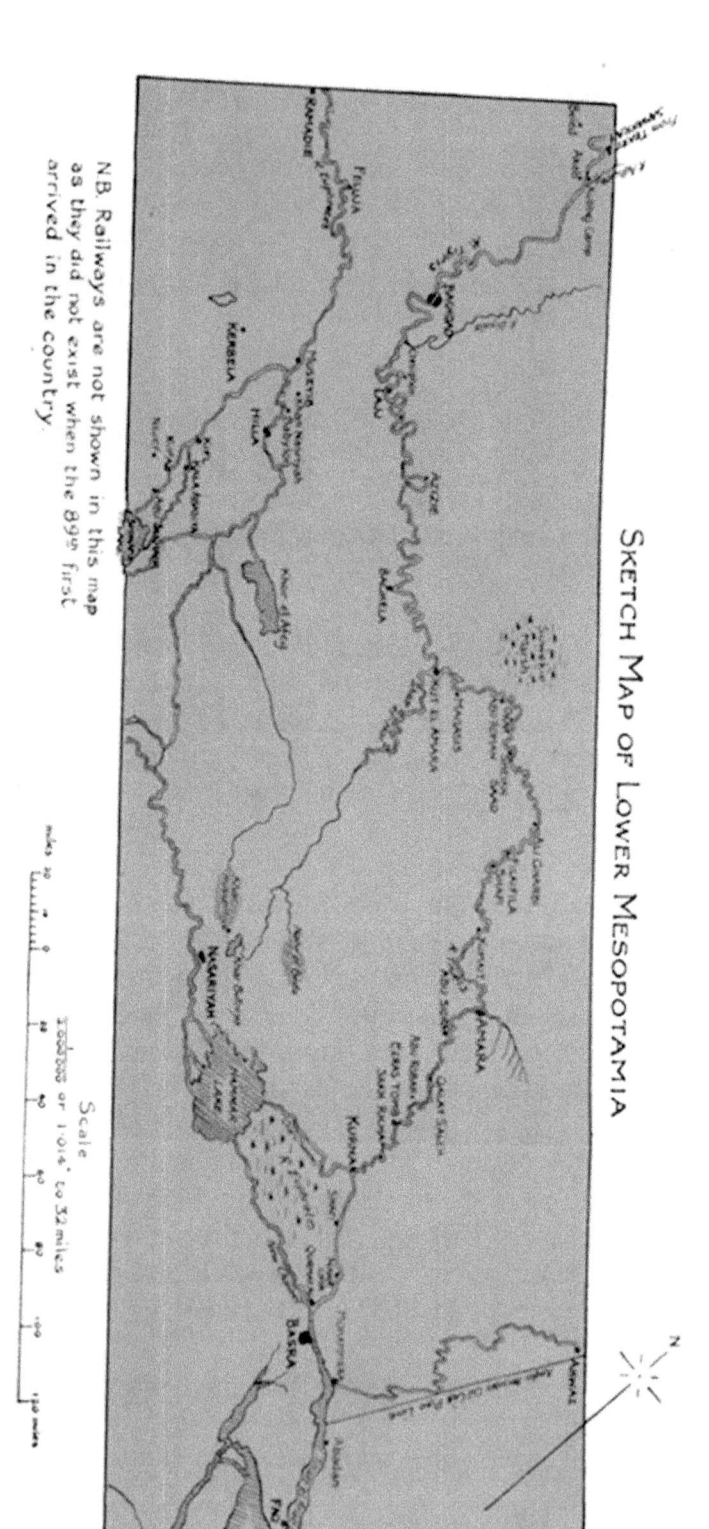

Sketch Map of Lower Mesopotamia

N.B. Railways are not shown in this map as they did not exist when the 89th first arrived in the country.

then dashed out and was fired at, but luckily only wounded in the shoulder.

The *Shabanas* then bolted, followed by the guard, who had turned out at the noise of firing. Captain Marshall had some few days previously moved the guard from a room near the gateway to a small room at the other end of the courtyard. The guard commander found it impossible to fire, as he did not know whom to fire at; the escaping *Shabanas* had, up till then, always been looked upon as friends. Also, other sepoys of the platoon who had gone outside when the gates were opened at 0600 hours and who were now streaming back, alarmed by the noise of the firing, effectually masked their fire.

Captain Hampson then took command and, with the assistance of the guard, closed the gates of the Serai. An hour later, one squadron 10th Lancers, one section 13-pounder Q.F. guns, and two platoons of the 89th Punjabis moved out from Kufa, and took up a position to the east and south-east of Nejef, in support of Marshall's Serai. Subedar Allah Ditta taking up a position with his platoon on a ridge close to the city walls, found himself subjected to a very hot fire. But the Subedar showed such coolness that he inspired his men with confidence, so that they were soon masters of the situation n by their superiority of fire.

Owing to the sacred shrine at Nejef, it was not possible to treat the city with any degree of severity, for fear of violating the religious principles of millions of people .

Captain Campbell-Balfour, the Senior Political Officer of the district with utter disregard for his own safety, and taking only a small escort of Shabanas, entered Nejef city at 0900 hours, to make inquiries as to the attitude of the chief sheikhs and other inhabitants. At 1200 hours, he returned safely, and, though under fire from the walls of the city, coolly walked back to Marshall's Serai (as it was now to be named). Battalion Headquarters were now established at Tramway Post, half-way between Kufa and Nejef. Captain J. S. Hannah was sent up with one platoon of C Company to reinforce the platoon already in Marshall's Serai.

After Captain Campbell-Balfour's return from Nejef, Lieutenant-Colonel Geoghegan, being the senior officer on the spot, decided to blockade the city until the murderers were surrendered. The first step was to cut off their water supply.

Besides a little water which flows underground and was obtainable at various holes (or *karezes*), the chief supply was from a canal about twelve feet broad, which led away from the Euphrates, near Abu Sikhair Post, right up to the south-western corner of the city. This supply was closed by the garrison of Abu Sikhair Post.

In the afternoon, the Brigade Commander arrived and took over the area, but left Lieutenant-Colonel Geoghegan in command of the situation at Nejef. The latter selected for his Headquarters a point about a mile along the tramway towards Kufa from Marshall's Serai. This was known as Blockade Headquarters.

At first, owing to the lack of numbers, it was only possible to ensure a "blockade" by means of day and night patrols around the city. This was found unsatisfactory, as many Arabs were able to slip in or out as they pleased. But, as reinforcements arrived, picquets were constructed round the city until, by March 24th, we had a complete cordon round Nejef, protected by a barbed wire entanglement. This cordon was gradually tightened until, in places, troops held positions actually on the walls and in the houses of the city itself. Eventually, the force under Lieutenant-Colonel Geoghegan, besides the 89th and the cavalry and guns already mentioned was composed of the following:-

1st/9th Middlesex Regiment; 2½ Companies 1st/4th Somersets; 1½ Companies 1/3rd Gurkhas; 1 Company 8th Sappers and Miners; 1 Section 6-inch Howitzers of 150th Battery; 1½ Sections No.207 Machine Gun Company ; and 1 Section L.A.M. Battery

On the morning of March 22nd a party of Nejefis attempted to burn the gate of Marshalls Serai, but were driven off with grenades and rifle fire.

Later in the day, a deputation of sheikhs from Nejef was informed of our terms, which would have to be complied with before the blockade could be lifted. They were as follow:-

    1 A fine of Rs50,000.

    2 A fine of 1,000 rifles.

    3 Certain prominent men, and the murderers of Captain Marshall, to be surrendered unconditionally.

    4 A hundred persons from the rebel quarter of the city to be deported as prisoners of war.

A large number of Arabs were now being caught daily trying to leave or enter the city, and it was evident that the blockade was being felt. Water was very scarce, and prices of food were soaring high. From March 25th onwards, the situation grew daily quieter, and the fire from the city became very spasmodic.

On the night of March 31st/April 1st, a party of the enemy made a sortie, evidently with the idea of escaping through our line between Marshall's Serai and the picquet just south of it. They were, however, driven back again by heavy machine gun and rifle fire.

During March, our casualties were 1 sepoy killed and 4 wounded.

On April 6th, an aeroplane from Bagdad flew over Nejef, dropping leaflets stating our peace terms. The same day, news was received that Captain Hannah had been awarded the Military Cross for his gallantry in the defence of Marshall's Serai during the first two or three days of this show.

On the morning of April 7th, after a short bombardment carried out by the 6-in. howitzers, the 1st/3rd Gurkhas assaulted and took the Hawaish Mounds. These were high mounds of rubbish, etc., not unlike the slag-heaps which one sees in any mining district. They were close to the south-western corner of the walls of Nejef and, of late, much sniping had been carried out from them by the enemy. After this, there was no more resistance on the part of the inhabitants, but it was not until May 4th that the terms were fully complied with, and the blockade raised.

On the 13th, the detachment of H Company (which was now· at

Kala Abbaisyeh instead of Kifl), and on the 14th the detachment of F Company at Abu Sikhair, were both relieved by the 1st/3rd Gurkhas, so that the Battalion was all together again.

On May 2nd, Major J. D. Crawford, D.S.O., M.C., rejoined us but was not allowed to stay with us for long, as he was recalled for duty on the staff five days later. Immediately after the raising of the blockade of Nejef the 89th were moved to Kubbej, a camp on the left bank of the Tigris, opposite Akab, where the remainder of the Brigade was now being concentrated.

Here took over an outpost line from the 94th Infantry and the 25th Punjabis, but no one quite understood what kind of enemy might be expected, unless it were marauding tribes from the north.

At first, we garrisoned this outpost line with two companies. This was later reduced to one company, and finally, after four or five weeks, was abandoned altogether.

We now enjoyed a period of real organised training, of which we were all badly in need. On May 16th, the Battalion was depleted of a whole company. Lieutenant J. S. Hannah, M.C., Second Lieutenant C. E. Morton, and C Company left us to go and form part of the 1st/153rd Infantry.

All records of the old C Company in the Depot in India, with its corresponding personnel, clerks, recruits, etc., were also transferred to the depot of the newly-formed battalion. To take the place of C Company, another company was formed by transferring non-commissioned officers and men from the three remaining companies.

This new company was composed of two platoons, Punjabi Mussalmans, one of Sikhs, and one of Brahmans.

It is very gratifying to know that Hannah and his company acquitted themselves with great credit. Several British officers who had anything to do with them having written their appreciation to the Commandant at one time or another.

On June 4th, H Company was sent on detachment to a camp near the railway station at Beled.

On June 8th, Captain Puri, I.M.S., joined the Battalion as Medical Officer in relief of Lieutenant Sondhi, M.C., I.M.S., who proceeded on leave to India; and ten days later, Lieutenant T. J. Rogers and Second Lieutenant H. R. F. Tweedy reported their arrival.

In the middle of June, the 1914 pattern Ross rifle, with which the Battalion had been equipped on arrival in Mesopotamia, was done away with, and, in exchange, we were re-equipped with the S.L.E. rifle.

Also, at the end of May and during June, small drafts arrived in driblets. These were chiefly composed of those men who had been left behind in Karachi, in isolation for mumps.

On July 27th, orders were received for the Battalion to move to Samarrah (a distance of some thirty miles), and at the same time to construct a road to that place from Kubbej.

This "road-making" consisted chiefly of marking out the existing Arab highway with two parallel lines of *burjis* (mounds of earth) but included the construction of bridges and culverts over *nullahs*, so that transport might use the road at any season of the year. The construction of this road was carried out entirely by the Battalion in accordance with detailed instructions issued by an officer of the Royal Engineers.

To avoid the heat of the day, the men worked from 0300 until 0800 hours and again from 1800 until 2000 hours. Only three companies were available as H Company, at Beled, moved direct to Samarrah by rail, and prepared the camp there for the Battalion.

Work was begun on July 29th, but was not completed until August 14th. On August 13th, the Battalion took over all guards and duties in and around Samarrah, so as to allow the units of the 54th Brigade their full personnel whilst carrying out battalion and brigade training.

On August 30th, F Company, with a party of ten sappers and miners, left the Battalion to tow forty-six pontoons up the river to Tekrit. This sounds an easy task, but in reality there were many difficulties to overcome. First of all, the bed of the Tigris above Samarrah is pebbly, and whenever a canvas pontoon was allowed to scrape on the ground it at once sprang a leak. Secondly, where the banks of the river were high and the water below deep, the pontoons had to be rowed across to the other side. To overcome the first difficulty, the men towed their pontoons, wading the whole way in water two or three feet deep, and after the first day there were scarcely any leaks reported; and, to overcome the second difficulty, after the first day's towing, every man in F Company was given a lesson in the art of rowing. Each day, the last pontoon of all was manned by Sappers and Miners, who were constituted as a rescue party in case of need, being all good rowers. This party was called into use once to rescue Second Lieutenant Tweedy's topee, which fell into the river when that officer fell asleep whilst being rowed across the river.

On September 7th, 1918, we heard that the 89th, together with several other Indian battalions, had been selected to go to yet another front-this time Salonika.

On September 27th, the Battalion commenced its journey to Salonika, entraining at Samarrah for Bagdad. Basrah was reached on the morning of October 6th, and here we had to wait for three days. On the afternoon of October 9th, all stores were loaded on H.T. *Aronda*, on to which the British officers also embarked, while the men remained in bivouacs on the wharf. The next morning, they also embarked, and we sailed immediately for Fao. Here early on the 11th we transhipped on to H.T. *Indarra*, an Australian coastal pleasure steamer, in which British officers were installed in most comfortable roomy state-rooms. The transhipment was a lengthy business, as proper gangways were not available, and, although it was completed by the afternoon, we did not get away until the next day.

On October 19th, the *Indarra* called at Aden. Some of us took the opportunity of landing and going to pay a visit to our old friends of the 69th, who were then stationed there. Sailing the same afternoon, we arrived at Port Said on the 26th. Here, for various reasons, we were held up for six days. Men were allowed ashore, and on one occasion the whole Battalion landed in the ship's boats and went for a route march. On this occasion, F Company provided the crews for the boats, and the rowing practice they had had on the Tigris early in September was put to a practical use.

On November 1st, the *Indarra* put to sea in convoy with nine other ships, escorted by one British and three Japanese destroyers. Late in the afternoon of the first day out, we passed near, and one of our escort was able to pick up, two French airmen who had made a forced landing in the sea the night before whilst searching for enemy submarines which had been reported. We were only just in time to save them, as their seaplane was almost entirely submerged, and was then sinking fast.

The next day we had the excitement of an enemy submarine attack, but fortunately nothing came of it, as the submarine happened to emerge close to one of our escort. Two destroyers went for the enemy at full speed, and, as he had immediately submerged again, dropped five or six depth charges, but were unable to claim a hit, as no signs of oil or wreckage appeared.

At last we reached Salonika at 1900 hours on November 4th. The next day, we disembarked and marched out to Ushanter Camp, where we settled down to the usual training, and prepared to go "up the line". The news of the Armistice was received on the evening of November 11th with a mad salvo of Verey lights, flares and discharge of rifles and revolvers. Sad to relate, the soldier-driver of the British C.-in-C. was killed by a stray bullet. The Indians took the news of the Armistice more stoically, the Subedar-Major asking if the men had permission to cheer!

Chapter IX
Salonika And The Army Of The Black Sea
November 1918 To October 1920

After the Armistice we settled down to a quiet life of ordinary daily parades and camp life. On November 18th, 7 officers and 13 non-commissioned officers from British regiments joined the Battalion for duty. This was in accordance, with a scheme for "stiffening" those Indian battalions which were sent to Salonika.

However, before very long, most of these officers and non-commissioned officers left us to get demobilised. Only one officer, Lieutenant Faithorne, remained with us for any length of time. Then he, too, left us in 1921 to return to his own regiment soon after the 89th returned to India.

Leave to the United Kingdom was now opened for British officers, and were re all considerably cheered at the thought of at least three weeks at home sooner or later.

Christmas Day came, and was celebrated in as fitting a manner as possible. It is understood that an eye-witness saw many British officers walking arm-in-arm and singing songs, visiting each battalion mess in turn. But it was after dinner, and too much stress should not be laid on the veracity of the witness.

On the 28th, the Battalion embarked on H.M.T. *Malwa*, and sailed the next afternoon for Batoum, an important place, being the port for delivering to Europe the oil from the oilfields at Baku.

On arrival in Batoum we found the country in a very disturbed state; in fact, it remained so, and could only be considered safe wherever British or Indian troops happened to be. The only disciplined troops we found on our arrival were Turks, who were being rapidly evacuated as fast as ships could be supplied to take them back to Constantinople.

The British Mission and Headquarters of the 27th Division, on their arrival moved without delay to Tiflis to try to bring their influence to bear on the Georgian Government, who were then at war with Armenia. This "war" was stopped by a subaltern of a Scottish regiment, who drove up between the two armies flying the Union Jack on his car. Calling up the opposing commanders, he told them to go back home, which they eventually did

Early on January 8th, the Battalion, which had entrained at a siding the night before, started off in one long train, with the idea of posting garrisons at places of importance on the railway between Batoum and Tiflis. Two Russian officers accompanied Battalion Headquarters, to act as interpreters and to advise as to the military importance of the various places en route. A depot, including the regimental transport and heavy kit, was left behind at Batoum.

All went well until the train reached Supsa (Georgian territory), where the attitude of the Georgian troops was distinctly hostile. However, leaving one platoon here, the rest of us continued our journey to Samtredi. Here the situation was found to be impossible, so, to avoid friction with the Georgians, the Commanding Officer decided to proceed direct to Tiflis and report.

On arrival in Tiflis, a full report was made to the 81st Brigade Head-quarters and the British Mission, who at once got into touch with the Georgian Government.

Nothing could be done in a hurry, however, and it was not until six days later, that we started back to complete the posting of our garrisons. This time the Commanding Officer was accompanied by a senior officer of the staff of General Kuriloff, commanding Georgian railways, so that no difficulty was experienced, and, finally, three companies were split up in seventeen detachments on bridges and tunnels, with Battalion Headquarters and a reserve company at Mickhailovo.

During these early months we had to endure a considerable amount of cold weather, and detachments were at times employed in clearing snow from points and lines, as we had heavy falls of snow in many places.

A few petty incidents with Georgian troops occurred. One or two of our sentries were fired at and wounded. Finally, the following incident, which rather discouraged them to play any more tricks with us, happened on March 15th. While a troop train containing a Georgian battalion was passing slowly by our post at Sviri, some men in the train opened fire on the post, riddling the tents with bullet holes. The havildar in charge of the post blew the "Alarm" whistle and ordered two rounds rapid at the back of ,the disappearing train. Firing, in all, forty-six rounds, the post inflicted a severe lesson on the Georgians, killing two of them and wounding six (one severely). There were no casualties on our side.

On April 4th, orders were received, imposing upon us the duties of guarding all supply trains throughout the Caucasus. This included the whole line from Batoum to Baku and from Tiflis to Kars and Erivan. Our existing system was therefore scrapped, and the Battalion was distributed as follows :-

  A Company: Two platoons and Company Headquarters at Batoum, one platoon at Samtredi, one platoon at Kvirili.

  C Company: One platoon at Mickhailovo. Two platoons with Battalion Headquarters and Transport at Tiflis. One platoon at Akstafa.

  F Company: Two platoons at Tiflis. Two platoons and Company Headquarters at Alexandropol.

1. EAST FORT, BATOUM
2. ALEXANDER'S ARCHWAY, SALONIKA
3. THE PROMENADE, BATOUM
   Band of the Bedfordshire Light Infantry playing
4. "RED" BANNER Memento of Batoum

H Company: One platoon at Elisavetpol, one platoon at Evlaka one platoon at Adjikabal, one platoon and Company Headquarter at Baku.

These detachments were responsible for providing escorts for every supply train from their post to the next. Travelling in pairs, six or eight men were distributed the whole length of each train. They had to keep a look-out while the train was in motion, in case anyone might jump on while the train was moving slowly, and, when the train halted anywhere, their job was to hop out on each side of the train and prevent anyone coming near the train. After we instituted this system, not a single article was reported short on any train escorted by our men.

Leave for Indian ranks to India was now opened, and, on April 23rd, the first party of 2 Indian officers and 75 other ranks left Tiflis.

On the 10th a non-commissioned officer of F Company belonging to the detachment at Alexandropol was fired at by a Greek, who was taken prisoner and handed over to the A.P.M. at Tiflis.

The platoon of C Company at Akstafa was found to be unnecessary, and was withdrawn to Tiflis on May 16th. Two days later the Battalion had to supply an escort of I Indian officer and 20 other ranks, under Lieutenant Bates, for the G.O.C. Division, Major-General Cory, who went on a visit of inspection to Tabriz.

From the middle of the month we began handing over our train guard duties to the 2nd/6th Gurkhas, and on May 29th the whole Battalion was concentrated in camp just north-west of Tiflis, on the outskirts of the town. Hardly had we started on our field training and range practices than we were ordered to take over the train guard duties once more. This we did on June 17th, the garrisons being distributed in much the same way as before, the only big difference being that one section of F Company was sent to Alexandropol as guard on the R.T.O. at the station there.

On June 29th information was received that peace had been signed with Germany at 1514 hours the day before, in celebration of which, on the 30th, a salute of 101 guns was fired by the 99th Brigade R.F.A. at Tiflis.

A party of 2 Indian officers and 32 other ranks chosen from the Mussalmans left the Battalion on August 2nd to go under special arrangements on a pilgrimage to Mecca.

About this time it was decided, in view of the defeats of the White Russian armies on the Caspian and elsewhere, to evacuate Baku and Georgia and withdraw 10 Batoum. Shortly before this, an Italian Mission had travelled round the Caucasus with a view to Italy accepting a mandate for the country, but we heard later that they wisely declined President Wilson's suggestion.

Accordingly, on August 26th, all detachments beyond Tiflis were withdrawn, while the evacuation of Tiflis began on September 2nd. Detachments at intermediate stations between Tiflis and Batoum were collected en route, and we all arrived at Batoum safely, late in the evening of the 3rd. Next day we detrained and went under canvas in East Fort. After several weeks, we all moved into comfortable barracks close to East Fort

In Batoum, the 89th had to find guards for many banks, as well as for ammunition dumps and other places of military importance. The reliefs paraded over 120 strong every day. This put a severe strain on the men, who had to endure it for many months. Later on, duties were cut down to a minimum, but owing to leave parties in India, and detachments elsewhere, the situation was never relieved to any great extent.

We also had to find garrisons for posts at Kedi and Khoulo, and at Artvin and Artenuch. At first garrisons for these places were found by one platoon under a British officer at the first two, and the same for the other two places. As required by the situation, these garrisons were increased and decreased. At one time there was a platoon at each place and a fifth at Borchka.

Major Scruby, who had been temporarily in command of the 84th Punjabis at Baku for the past three months, returned to us on October 22nd, and on September 14th went on leave to England, taking with him Havildar Shahmed Khan to be decorated with his Victoria Cross by His Majesty the King Emperor.

On the 12th, and again on the 31st, one of our sentries (in each case an F Company man and at a lonely spot) was sniped at and wounded by some unknown assailant.

During December many parties left for India, and the first parties which had gone from Tiflis in April began drifting back again. Shahmed Khan V.C., and his orderly returned from England, and the Mecca party also returned very pleased with their excursion.

During these winter months, British officers, and others who had guns, were able to indulge in some capital rough shooting round about Batoum. On Christmas Day, to work off a heavy lunch, two British officers went out for three hours, bringing back a bag containing, duck, snipe, woodcock, teal, golden plover, and pigeon, about twelve head of game altogether At the end of March, owing to rumours of the British evacuation of Batoum Province, the Georgian Army concentrated at points on the borders of the province. Consequently, our detachments up the Kedi and Artvin roads were increased, and, in the middle of April, F Company, under Captain Rennick, together with one section of 18-pdr. guns, were sent to Kobuleti to persuade the main Georgian Army to get out of Batoum Province. This they did after several Gilbertian incidents.

At the end of April and for the whole of May, C Company was billeted in the town (two platoons at the main police station, and two platoons and Company Headquarters with the A.P.M.) to help the local Russian police to maintain order in the town.

Nothing further of any great importance occurred until July 8th, when Batoum was finally handed over to the Georgians. Eight hundred men of our naval and military forces participated in the handing over ceremony. Two hundred naval ratings, two hundred Marines, two hundred men of the 2nd Bn. Durham Light Infantry, and two hundred of the 89th marched through the town with fixed bayonets, to the tune of *Marching through Georgia*, played by the massed bands and buglers of the Navy and the Durham Light

Infantry.

An old Russian General who was watching the ceremony, and seeing the steadiness and precision with which our detachments wheeled into and halted at their places in the square, turned to our General Officer Commanding, Brigadier-General Cooke Collis, C.M.G., and remarked: 'Ah, I have never admired your men so much as I do today. Now I know why you British won the war.'

The next day we sailed for Constantinople. The Navy supplied us with a touching farewell by the band on one of their ships playing our March Past as we steamed out of the harbour. All the men on deck were called to Attention and, finally, three cheers were given for the Navy.

On July 12th, the ship arrived at Constantinople. The Battalion disembarked and marched through Pera into a standing camp (Nissen huts) just outside Chichli.

We now found ourselves under the command of Brigadier-General Beckwith, who, though he pointed out many of our shortcomings when we first arrived, expressed himself very satisfied with the high standard of efficiency of the Battalion before we left his command, two months later.

Another small party of Mussalmans left on a pilgrimage to Mecca on July 16th, and leave parties to India continued to be despatched, while former ones rejoined us.

On September 14th, 1920, leaving A and H Companies at Chichli, under Captain Ledgerwood, and three other British officers, the remainder of the 89th embarked on H.T. *Karadeniz* for Bombay.

A and H Companies remained in Chichli Camp until suitable transport became available on October 5th, when they also embarked for India, arriving at Kamptee on November 3rd 1920.

Thus the battalion united once more, was able to look back with satisfaction on six years of active service, during which all ranks had unfailingly upheld the best traditions of the Indian Army.

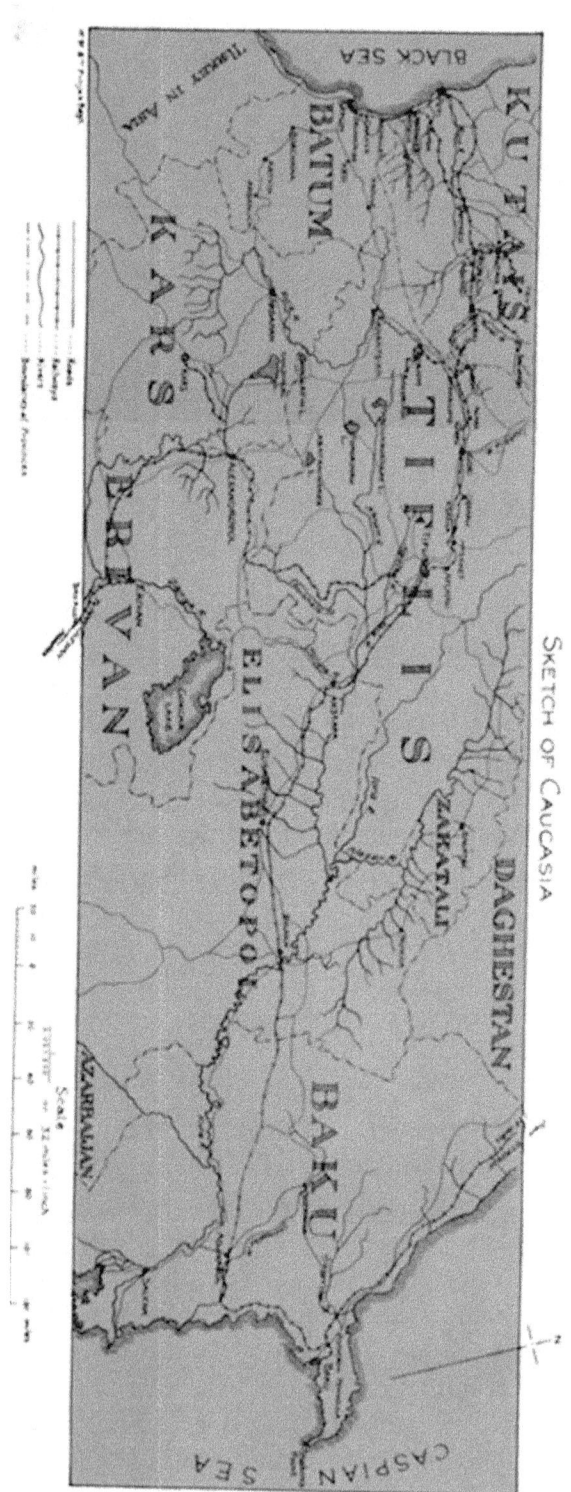

Appendix I

Marching-Out Strength of the 89th Punjabis on Leaving Dinapore on October 27th, 1914

British Officers	13
Indian Officers	16
Indian Other Ranks	805

The British Officers included:-

Lieut Colonel L. W. Y. Campbell	Commandant.
Lieut Colonel E. R. B. Murray	Second-in-Command.
Major W. S. Prentis	D.C. Commander
Major N. M. Geoghegan	D.C. Commander
Captain P. Wood	D.C. Commander
Captain W. S. J. Scruby	M.G. and Signalling Officer
Captain R. S. Engledue	D.C. Officer.
Captain J. D. Crawford	Adjutant.
Lieut G. E. Masters	D.C. Officer.
Lieut H. T. Rohde	Quartermaster.
2 Lieut M. H. A. Campbell	D.C. Officer.
Captain Fielding, I.M.S.	Medical Officer

Captain J. D. Strong, 90th Punjabis. Joined in Karachi as D.C. Officer

Appendix II

Copy of a Memo. No. OX23D1. 18/2/1915
From C.S.O. Canal Defence H.Q.
To the G.O.C. 29th Brigade

I am directed to request that you will convey to the Officers and men under your command the G.O.C.-in-Chief's high appreciation of the work done by them during the recent operations.

The conduct of the troops was excellent, and the G.O.C. in C., in expressing his satisfaction at the results of the recent engagements, congratulates all ranks on their successes which have necessitated the retirement of Djemal Pasha's Army at any rate for the time being. He is confident, should the enemy's attack be renewed, the result will be no less decisive.

Appendix III

Copy of a Wire
From the G.O.C. in C., Egypt
To the G.O.C Alexandria.

A/186. Please inform Officers Commanding 69th Punjabis and 89th Punjabis that their Battalions have been selected to reinforce the Expeditionary Forces in France, and that as soon as arrangements can be made they will proceed there

I congratulate these two distinguished Regiments on having been selected.

    MAXWELL
    CAIRO
    18th May, 1916.

Appendix IV

Indian Army Corps.

Order Of The Day No. 10.

Dated 29th April, 1916.

The Corps Commander desires to place on record his very high appreciation of the good services rendered on the night of 17th/18th April by Major-General H. D. U. Keary and the troops under his command when they, supported by the 13th Division, successfully withstood the furious onslaught and successive counter-attacks by the 2nd and 35th Turkish Divisions from 7pm 17th to dawn 18th April. During this stand the following units specially distinguished themselves – 3rd Mountain Battery; 66th and 14th Batteries, R.F.A.; Connaught Rangers; No.2 Company, Manchesters; 27th Punjabis; 47th Sikhs; 59th Rifles; and 59th Punjabis.

Great credit is also due to Major-General Maude and the 13th Division for the prompt action taken and arrangements made to meet the urgent calls for support from the 3rd Division.

[EXTRACT]

Appendix V

Special Order by Major-General R. G. EGERTON, C.B.

Commanding 71 (Ferozepore) Brigade,

10/5/16

On relinquishing the command of the Ferozepore Brigade, which he has held for four and a half years, Major-General Egerton offers to all ranks his most grateful thanks for the work which they have constantly performed, especially since landing in France in September, 1914

To the 89th Punjabis who have served with him in France and Mesopotamia, General Egerton offers his heartiest thanks for the gallant work they have invariably done.

[EXTRACT]

Appendix VI

Farewell Orders to The Battalion, on Leaving Mesopotamia
August, 1916

On the departure of the 89th Punjabis I wish to place on record my high appreciation of the splendid work this Regiment has done during its association with the Division Both in France and Mesopotamia all ranks have acquitted themselves with the greatest credit, Officers and men alike, proving their eagerness to take on any work, however difficult or dangerous. In raids and patrols, the subordinate commanders have displayed initiative and courage, while in larger affairs all ranks have shown dash and determination in the face of opposition and often heavy losses worthy of the highest praise.

Throughout, the conduct and discipline of the Regiment has been of the best, while the leading and handling have left nothing to be desired. My thanks are due to Lieut-Colonel Geoghegan for the able manner he has commanded and t the other Officers for their loyal support and assistance.

This Regiment has had the unique experience of having fought in four of the main theatres of the war – Egypt (including Red Sea), Gallipoli, France and Mesopotamia and I am given to understand has acquitted itself equally wall in all four

In wishing all ranks farewell. I again wish to express my satisfaction of the services of the Regiment

30th July 1916.

(Sd) H. D. Keary, Major-General,
      Commanding 3rd (Lahore) Division

Extract of 7 Brigade Special Order
Dated 30th July 1916

From the end of May, 1915, to the departure of the Indian Corps from France, the 89th served in France, beginning here their association with the 7th Brigade, and both in that country and in Mesopotamia they have borne a full share in all the fighting the Brigade has taken part in. They have gained a well-earned reputation for steadfast gallantry and reliability, while in soldierly efficiency they have been a pattern of what a Regiment should be.

Appendix VII

Marching Out Strength of the 1/89th Punjabis
on Leaving Nowshera for Mesopotamia
26th September, 1917.

British Officers	23
Indian Officers	20
Indian Other Ranks	1,070
Followers	50

The following British and Indian Officers were included:-

Colonel L. W. Y. Campbell, C.M.G.	Commandant.
Lieut-Colonel N. M. Geoghegan	Second-in-Command
Major W. S. J. Scruby	Company Commander
Major R. S. Engledue	Company Commander
Captain M. H. A. Campbell	Adjutant
Lieut J. S. Hannah	Company Commander
Lieut R. B. Dawkes	Company Officer
Lieut H. P. S. Bullock	Company Officer
2 Lieut G. C. Hele	Company Officer
2 Lieut R. C. S. Bates	Quartermaster
2 Lieut C. E. Morton	Company Officer
2 Lieut H. N. H. Dick	Company Officer
Lieut S. D. Sondhi, M.C., I.M.S.	Medical Officer

Subedar-Major Sunder Singh Bahadur

Subedars	**Jemadars**
Allayhar Khan	Kishun Singh
Saide Khan	Jiwan Singh
Jasmal Singh	Kirpal Singh
Gulab Khan	Bagga Singh, I.D.S.M

Bishun Datt Dube
Allah Ditta
Rure Khan.
Waryam Singh.
Rampershad Tiwari.
Ramji Misr, I.D.S.M
Nur Muhammed.
Ghulam Muhammed, I.D.S.M.

Baldeo Singh, I.D.S.M.
Sultan Singh
Bur Singh, I.D.S.M.

Appendix VIII

Roll Of Honour.

The following casualties were sustained by the Battalion from 1914 to 1918

	British Officers	Indian Officers	Other Ranks	Total
Killed or died of wounds	5	4	137	146
Wounded	14	14	762	790
Missing, presumed killed	1	1	62	64
Prisoners of war		1	16	17
			Total	1017

British Officer casualties included:

Killed or Died of Wounds:
Captain E. J. Burdett (11th Rajputs)   Captain P. Wood
Captain H. T. Rohde   3 Lieut S. V. Hasluck
2 Lieut H. O. C. Bates

Missing, presumed killed   Lieut G. E. Masters

Wounded:
Colonel L. W. Y. Campbell, C.M.G (twice)   Major W. S. Prentis
Major N. M. Geoghegan (twice) Captain W. S. J. Scruby
Major R. S. Engledue (three times)   Captain W. L. B. Chapman
Captain R. F. D. Barnett, M.C.   Captain J. D. Strong
Captain W. R. James   Lieut H. H. Greene
2 Lieut H. Humphrey   2 Lieut V. F. C. Peto
2 Lieut M. H. A. Campbell   2 Lieut P. A. Denny

Indian Officer casualties included
Killed or Died of Wounds:
Subedar Chainchal Singh   Subedar Zaman Shab, I.O.M.
Jemadar Jagdam Singh   Jemadar Ramdhyan Tiwari.

Missing, presumed killed   Jemadar Ramsurat Misr,

Prisoner of war   Jemadar Khan Muhammed

Wounded:
Subedar-Major Sunder Singh Bahadur
Subedar Saide Khan   Subedar Subha Singh
Subedar Bakshish Singh   Subedar Fakir Muhammed (twice).
Jemadar Kesar Shah   Jemadar Bagga Singh, I.D.S.M
Jemadar Kushun Singh   Jemadar Madat Khan
Jemadar Jiwan Singh   Jemadar Zaman Khan
Jemadar Dhanna Singh   Jemadar Rure Khan
Jemadar Gainda Singh

Appendix IX

List of Honours And Awards

Victoria Cross:
Naik Shahmed Khan

C.M.G
Brigadier-General L W. Y. Campbell.

D.S.O.
Lieut-Colonel N. M. Geoghegan.
Major D. Crawford   Major W. C. K. Bro
Lieut-Colonel W. S. Prentis (whilst commanding 72nd Panjabi),

O.B.E. (Military)
Major W. S. J. Scruby   Captain M. H. A Campbell
Lieut. H P. S. Bullock

Military Cross
Captain R. F. D. Burnett (42nd Deolis)
Captain J.D. Crawford.   Captain W. R. James
Captain S. D. Sondhi, I.M.S   Lieut J. Hannah

Order of British India (2nd Class)
Subedar-Major Sunder Singh.

Indian Order of Merit (2nd Class)
Subedar Zaman Shah   Jemadar Rampersan Tiwari
Havildar Hira Tiwari   Havildar Mahtab Ali
Naik Indar Singh   Naik Suleiman

Indian Distinguished Service Medal
Subadar Allah Ditta
Jemadar Bagga Singh
Havildar Ramji Mist
Havildar Harnam Single

Jemadar Bur Singh
Havildar Baldeo Singh
Havildar Ghulam Muhammed

Havildar Jagdoo Dube
Havildar Gurdit Singh
Naik Mohd Khan
Sepoy Der Singh
Sepoy Indar Singh,
Sepoy Narain Singh
Sepoy Amur Dad
Sepoy Mit Singh
Sepoy Kishun Singh.
Sepoy Sher Muhammed
Sepoy Dassunda Singh

Havildar Mohd Sadiq

Naik Karm Dad
Sepoy Buta Singh
Sepoy Waryam Singh
Sepoy Santa Singh
Sepoy Ramadahin Tiwari
Sepoy Hazura Singh
Sepoy Harnam Singh
Sepoy Mehr Singh

Indian Meritorious Service Medal

Jemadar Sakhi Muhammad
Havildar Fateh Khan
Havildar Nizam Din
Havildar Chirag Din
Havildar Janki Singh
Havildar Taj Mohd
Havildar Ram Sarup Singh
Havildar Amar Singh
Naik Fateh Ali
Naik Musaddi Singh
Naik Sirenewas Misr
Naik Chanda Singh
Sepoy Hashmat Ali
Sepoy Gauhr Din

Jemadar Teja Singh
Havildar Sheorattan Singh
Havildar Harnam Singh
Havildar Kisbun Singh
Havildar Harnam Singh
Havildar S. Joseph
Havildar Balwant Singh

Naik Hukm Dad.
Naik Sawaya Singh
Naik Isher Singh
Naik Saudager Khan
Sepoy Rukan Din
Sepoy Nawab Khan

Award of Brevet Rank
Colonel   Lieut-Colonel L. W. Y Campbell, C.M.G
Lieutenant-Colonel   Major J. D. Crawford D.SO, M.C.

Major   Captain R. S. Engledue

Mentions
Tigris Corps Order of the Day No. 10, dated 29/4/16
The 89th Punjabis

Despatches
Captain W. G. K. Broome
Lieut H. P. S. Bullock
Captain R. F. D. Burnett (42 Deoli Regt.)
Lieut-Colonel L. W. Y. Campbell (four times)
Lieut M. H. A. Campbell (twice)
Captain J. D. Crawford (six times)
Captain R. S. Engledue (twice)
Major N. M. Geoghegan (five times)
2 Lieut S. V. Hasluck
Captain W. R. James
Lieut G. E. Masters
Captain H. R. Pelly
Lieut-Colonel W. S. Prentis
Major W. S. J. Scruby (twice)
Captain P. Wood

Subedar-Major Sunder Singh   Subedar Kirpal Singh
Subedar Allayar Khan   Subedar Sheobaksh Singh
Subedar-Major Saide Khan   Subedar Bur Singh
Subedar Gulab Khan (twice).   Subedar Ghulam Muhammed
Subedar Rure Khan   Jemadar Teja Singh (twice)
Jemadar Jiwan Singh.

290 Sepoy Bur Singh   1998 Havildar Narain Singh
457 Havildar Feroze Khan   2028 Sepoy Buta Singh
1218 Bug-Major Bahadur Singh   2106 Nail Isher Singh
1279 Havildar Inayatullah Khan   2121 Sepoy Pala Singh
1343 Sepoy Mehr Singh   2131 Sepoy Dasaunda Singh
1585 Havildar (later Jemadar)
2225 Lance-Naik Baghel Singh Sakhi Muhammed
2254 Havildar Chiragh Bin   1605 Naik (afterwards Subedar)

2316 Sepoy Indar Singh Shahmed Khan V.C.
2416 Sepoy Narain Singh   1653 Havildar Gurditt Singh
2494 Sepoy Harnam Singh   1654 Havildar Harnam Singh
2578 Sepoy Sher Muhammed   1766 Havildar (afterwards Jemadar)
1720 Sepoy Sandagar Khan Jagdeo Dube
2824 Sepoy Nawab Khan   1841 Naik Mahtab Ali
3207 Sepoy Harnam Singh
1903 Lance-Naik Wadhawa Singh (twice)
4397 Naik Fakir Singh

Serbian Decorations

Order of the White Eagle, 3rd Class (with swords)
Brig Gen L W. Y. Campbell, C.M.G

Order of the White Eagle 5th Class (with Swords)
Major J. D. Crawford M.C.

Serbian Silver Medal
Havildar Nur Mohd

Russian Order of St George 2nd Class
Naik Shahmed Khan V.C.

Jagirs 2

Special Grants of Land or Pensions in Lieu 27

Appendix X

Nominal Roll of Combatant British Officers

Who Served With the 1/89th Punjabis

During The Great War, 1914–18

Bampfield, Lieut G. C. (90th Punjabis).

Barnes, 2 Lieut W. C. (I.A.R.O.)
Bates 2 Lieut H. O. C. (I.A.R.O.)
Bates 2 Lieut (Capt) R. C. S.

Broome Capt W.G.K.
Bullock 2 Lieut (Lieut) H. P. S. (I.A.R.O.)
Burdett Capt E. J. (11th Rajputs)
Burnett Capt R. F. D. (42nd Deolis)

Campbell Lt-Col (Colonel) L. W. Y.
Campbell 2 Lieut (Lieut) M. H. A.
Chapman Capt (Major) W. L. B.

Coner Capt H. (112th Infantry)

Crawford Capt (Major) J. D.
Davson Capt H. (82nd Punjabis)
Dawkins 2 Lieut (Capt) R. B. (I.A.R.O.)
Dick 2 Lieut H. N. H. (I.A.R.O.)
Engledue Capt (Major) R.S.
Faithorme Lieut H. (Salonika)
Geoghegan Major (Lt-Col) N. M.
Gething Lieut L. R. (I.A.R.O.)
Greene Lieut H. H. (I.A.R.O.)
Green Lieut P. A. (I.A.R.O.)

Hannah Lieut (Capt.) J. S. (I.A.R.O.)
Hasluck 2 Lieut S. V. (I.A.R.O.)

Hele 2 Lieut (Capt) G, C. (I.A.R.O.)

Humphrey 2 Lieut (Lieut.) H. (I.A.R.O.)
Ivens Lieut (Salonika)
James Capt W. R.
Ledgerwood Lieut (Capt) F. H. (I.A.R.O)
Martelli Capt (I.A.R.O.)
Masters Lieut G. E.
McCutcheon Capt J. (Salonika)
Milne 2 Lieut (Lieut) E. M. (I.A.R.O.)
Morton 2 Lieut (Lieut) C. E.
Murray Lt-Col E. R .B.
O'Reilly 2 Lieut (Lieut.) K.W.R. (I.A.R.O.)
Peto 2 Lieut (Lieut) V. F. C. (I.A.R.O.)
Philips 2 Lieut P. J.
Prentis Major W. S.
Price 2 Lieut H. A. (Salonika)
Rennick 2 Lieut (Capt) G. B.
Rogers 2 Lieut (Capt) T. J.
Rohde Lieut H. T.
Scruby Capt (Major) W. S. J.
Strong Capt J. D. (90thPunjabis)
Tweedy 2 Lieut (Lieut) H. R. F
Wadley 2 Lieut (Capt) G. C. L. (I.A.R.O.)
White Lieut (Salonika)
Wilcox Capt H. B. F. (91st Punjabis)
Wood Capt P.

NOTE: Where previous regiment or other information is not given the officer joined the Battalion from Sandhurst, Quetta, or Wellington (India).

The following Medical Officers also served with the Battalion:

Agarwal, Capt S. N., I.M.S.	Puri Capt I.M.S.
Allen, Lieut F. T. RAMC	Sondhi Capt S. D., I.M.S
Fielding, Capt C. H., I.M.S.	Vankatachalam Capt K., I.M.S.

Appendix XI

Depot Notes.

The Depot remained at Dinapore from October 27th 1914, until September 2nd 1915, when it moved to Nowshera to rejoin the Battalion on its return from Mesopotamia. When the Battalion departed on active service a second time the Depot moved to Kamptee in early December, 1917.

The following officers commanded or served with the Depot at Dinapore

Captain W. L. B. Chapman.	Major W. S. Prentis
Captain W. R. James	Captain W. S. J. Scruby,
Major D. N. Stuart.	

The following officers commanded the Depot at Kamptee

Major W. L. B. Chapman	Captain G. C. L. Wadley,

and the following served with the Depot at Kamptee

Beer, Lieut G. E.	Kniveton, Lieut F.
Cangley, Lieut F. G., D.S.O., M.C	Ledgerwood, Lieut F. H.
Collins, Lieut F. T.	McCall, Lieut B.
Dance, Lieut E.	Parry, Lieut J. K
David, Lieut J.	Phillips, Lieut P. J.
De Freville, Lieut G. V.	Senior, Lient. T. B. G.
Gilbert, Lieut J. R.	Spence, Lieut J.
Hamilton, Lieut C. B.	Thorpe, Lient. J. A.
Hannington, Lieut A.	Tostevin, Lieut F. F.
Harrison, Lieut H. L.	Welbey, Lieut B. C.

Enlistments

From 1/11/1914 to 31/12/1914	43
During 1915	633
During 1916	602
During 1917	577
During 1918	849
During 1919	275
During 1920	95
Total	3074

Drafts
The following numbers were sent in drafts to the Battalion:

1915	194
1916	245
1918	343
1919	132
1920	70
Total	984

About the same number of men were sent in drafts to other Battalions. There is no record to show how many recruits were absorbed in the Battalion between September 1916, and November 1917 whilst the Battalion was stationed at Nowshera, but these would number perhaps 250.

www.ingramcontent.com/pod-product-compliance
Lightning Source LLC
Chambersburg PA
CBHW060048230426

43661CB00004B/709